FEUDALISM

in Egypt, Syria, Palestine and the Lebanon

1250 - 1900

A. N. POLIAK
M,A , PH.D

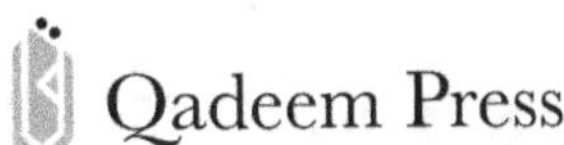

Qadeem Press

CONTENTS

PREFACE

THIS survey has a twofold purpose. Firstly, we have sought to supply the student of Arab history—as well as him who utilizes Arabic sources for philological or archæological studies—with a concise account of various feudal systems which existed in the countries and periods covered by our work, and with lists of principal technical terms relating to them, which are wanting as a rule in Arabic vocabularies. Secondly, we have aimed at providing the student of the modern Middle East with a key to such vestiges of feudal relations as are still traceable in these countries, including brief notes on the history of at least those prominent families the share of which in the feudal past was most remarkable.

My grateful thanks are due to the Council of the Royal Asiatic Society, under whose ægis this work is published.

PRINCIPAL SOURCES

ABŪ L-FIDĀ', *Ta'rīkh*. Constantinople, A.H. 1286 (always referred to as A. F.).

Id., *Taqwīm al-Buldān*, ed. Reinaud and de Slane. Paris, 1840.

ANONYM, *Geschichte der Mamlūkensultane in den Jahren 690–741 der Hiǵra*, ed. Zetterstéen. Leiden, 1919.

'AYN-I 'ALĪ MU'ADHDHINZĀDA, *Qawānīn-i Āl-i 'Uthmān*, Constantinople, A.H. 1280. French: Belin in *JA.*, 6e sér., xv (1870), pp. 239–288. German: P. A. von Tischendorf, *Das Lehnswesen in den Moslemischen Staaten*, Leipzig, 1872, pp. 56–103.

BERCHEM, MAX VAN, *Matériaux pour un Corpus Inscriptionum Arabicarum*. Paris, 1903–1930 (always referred to as *CIA.*).

DHAHABĪ, AL-, *Duwal al-Islām*. Hyderabad, A.H. 1337.

DIMISHQĪ, AL-, *Nukhbat al-Dahr*, ed. Mehren. St. Petersburg, 1886.

IBN 'ABD AL-ZĀHIR, *al-Alṭāf al-Khafiyya*, ed. Moberg. Lund, 1902.

IBN BAṬṬŪTA, *Tuḥfat al-Nuẓẓār*, ed. Defremery and Sanguinetti. Paris, 1893–1899.

IBN DUQMĀQ, *Kitāb al-Intiṣār*, ed. Vollers. Būlāq, 1893.

IBN ḤAJAR, *al-Durar al-Kāmina*. Hyderabad, A.H. 1348-1350.

IBN IYĀS, *Badā'i' al-Zuhūr*, vols. i, ii, iii, Būlāq, A.H. 1311–12 ; vols. iv, v, Istanbul, 1931–2.

IBN AL-JĪ'ĀN, *al-Tuhfa al-Saniyya*, ed. Moritz. Cairo, 1898.

IBN KHALDŪN, *Kitāb al-'Ibar*. Būlāq, A.H. 1284.

IBN AL-SHIḤNA, *al-Durr al-Muntakhab*. Beirut, 1909.

BN TAGHRĪ BIRDĪ, *al-Nujūm al-Zāhira*, ed. Popper. Berkeley, 1909, etc.,

Id., *Ḥawādith al-Duhūr*, ed. Popper. Berkeley, 1930.

Id., *al-Manhal al-Ṣāfī*, MSS. Paris, Slane 2068–2072.

IBN YAḤYĀ, ṢĀLIḤ, *Ta'rīkh Bayrūt*, 2nd ed. Beirut, 1927.

ISḤĀQĪ, AL-, *Akhbār al-Uwal*. Cairo, A.H. 1315.

JABARTĪ, AL-, *'Ajā'ib al-Āthār*. Cairo, A.H. 1297.

MAQRĪZĪ, AL-, *Khiṭaṭ*. Būlāq, A.H. 1270.

Id., *Sulūk*, Quatremère's translation and notes. Paris, 1837–1844.

MARITI, *Geschichte Fakkardins* (from the Italian). Gotha, 1790.

MICHAEL OF DAMASCUS, *Ta'rīkh Hawādith al-Shām wa-Lubnān*, ed. Ma'lūf. Beirut, 1912.

MUJĪR AL-DĪN, *al-Uns al-Jalīl*. Cairo, A.H. 1283.

NUWAYRĪ, AL-, *Nihāyat al-Arab*. Cairo, 1923–1935.

QALQASHANDĪ, AL-, *Ḍaw' al-Ṣubḥ*. Cairo, 1906.

Id., *Ṣubḥ al-A'shā*. Cairo, 1913–19.

Recueil de Firmans Impériaux Ottomans adressés aux Valis et aux Khédives d'Égypte. Cairo, 1934.

ROQUE, DE LA, *Voyage dans la Palestine, vers le Grand Emir.* 1718.

RUSTEM PASHA, *Die Osmanische Chronik* (abridg. transl. by L. Forrer). Leipzig, 1923.

RUSTUM, A. J., *Materials for a Corpus of Arabic Documents relating to the History of Syria under Mehemet Ali Pasha.* Beirut, 1930–4.

SAKHĀWĪ, AL-, *al-Ḍaw' al-Lāmi'.* Cairo, A.H. 1353–5.

SHIDYĀQ, AL-, *Akhbār al-A'yān fī Jabal Lubnān.* Beirut, 1859.

'UMARĪ, AL-, *Ta'rīf.* Cairo, A.H. 1312.

VOLNEY, C. F., *Voyage en Syrie et en Égypte.* Paris, 1787.

ẒĀHIRĪ, AL-, *Zubdat Kashf al-Mamālik,* ed. Ravaisse. Paris, 1894.

The following works are also often referred to :—

BOURON, N., *Les Druzes.* Paris, 1930.

CROMER, THE EARL OF, *Modern Egypt,* 2nd ed. London, 1911.

Égypte Moderne : I, J. J. MARCEL, *depuis la conquête des Arabes jusqu'à la domination française* ; II, A. RYME, *sous la domination française* III, P. ET H., *sous la domination de Méhémet Aly.* Paris, 1848.

FINN, J., *Stirring Times or Records from Jerusalem Consular Chronicles.* London, 1878.

GAUDEFROY-DEMOMBYNES, *La Syrie à l'époque des Mamelouks.* Paris, 1923.

HAMMER [-PURGSTALL], J. VON, *Geschichte der Osmanischen Reiches,* 2nd ed., Pest, 1834–6.

MAYER, L. A., *Saracenic Heraldry.* Oxford, 1933. Supplemented by *New Material for Mamlūk Heraldry* (*JPOS.,* xvii, 1937).

PERIODICALS

JA. = *Journal Asiatique.*

JPOS. = *Journal of the Palestine Oriental Society.*

JRAS. = *Journal of the Royal Asiatic Society.*

Ma. = *al-Mashriq.*

PEFQS. = *Palestine Exploration Fund Quarterly Statements.*

RÉI. = *Revue des Études Islamiques.*

ZDPV. = *Zeitschrift des Deutschen Palästina-Vereins.*

FEUDALISM IN EGYPT, SYRIA, PALESTINE, AND THE LEBANON, 1250–1900

I. The Feudal Troops of the Mamlūks

THE ruling caste of the Mamlūk state (1250–1517 = A.H. 648–923) was organized as feudal cavalry, consisting almost exclusively of foreigners of various origin; in the thirteenth and fourteenth centuries mostly natives of the Golden Horde, in the fifteenth and sixteenth centuries mostly Caucasians and especially Circassians.[1] All of them denoted themselves as " Turks ", since their common language, which distinguished them from the despised natives, was a Turkish dialect. The literature written in this language is poor [2] and almost unpublished, so that all studies relating to the Mamlūk state must be based upon the plentiful Arabic sources. It is necessary, however, to keep in mind that in regard to every non-Turkish technical term which we find in these sources a possibility exists of its being not the genuine term employed by the lords but only its more or less faithful translation, invented by their native clerks. All knights and emirs had to be, at least nominally,[3] Moslems.

This feudal army, commanded by an elected sultan,[4] consisted

---

[1] I have treated this question in *RÉI.*, 1935, pp. 231–248. Dimishqī, p. 264, l. 7, and Ibn Khaldūn, v, pp. 372–3, may be added to the sources enumerated there. The minority was of most heterogeneous stock, including West Europeans (*Sulūk*, I, i, p. 235 ; *Ḥawādith*, pp. 339, 591), and Jews (Sakhāwī, v, p. 197 ; Ibn Iyās, iv, p. 237).

[2] The study of this " Turkish " by natives was restrained by the unfavourable attitude of the rulers (Ẓāhirī, p. 99, ll. 20–1 ; Sakhāwī, vii, p. 160, No. 398), though those native clerks who overcame this difficulty had a particularly high standing.

[3] Cf. *Khiṭaṭ*, ii, p. 22, ll. 26–34, and Ibn Ḥajar, iii, p. 263, ll. 16–17.

[4] The title of sultan was inherited by the Ayyūbid and Mamlūk rulers from the Fāṭimid viziers (Bahā' al-Dīn Ibn Shaddād, ed. Cairo, A.H. 1346, p. 29, l. 1). The electoral body consisted of those " emirs of 100 " who resided in Cairo ; the preferred candidate was for the most part either a son of a former sultan or the Egyptian generalissimo (*atābak al-'asākir*). A Syrian governor-general could only capture the throne by a civil war, and controversies among the electors were also often settled in this way. After the election, the investiture by the caliph took place.

of three principal corps : (a) *ajnād al-ḥalqa*, i.e. the knights
who were in the sultan's service without being his freedmen ;
(b) the royal mamlūks, who were freedmen of the reigning
sultan (*mushtarawāt*), of the former sultans (*sulṭāniyya*) and
of dead emirs (*sayfiyya*) ; (c) the emirs and their mamlūks.[1]
As particular units within the first corps we may mention
(a) *al-baḥriyya*, viz. the descendants of the mamlūk corps of
the Ayyūbid sultan, al-Ṣāliḥ Ayyūb. Since Sultan Qalāūn
they became the guardians of gates of the citadel of Cairo
(which included the royal palace) and the bodyguards
of the sultan on his travels.[2] (b) *Al-ajnād al-qarānīṣ*, i.e.
those Caucasian noblemen who were not yet dubbed emirs,
but whose social position was already equal to that of
" emirs of 5 ".[3] Every hundred of *ajnād al-ḥalqa* were supervised by a *naqīb* and a *bāsh*, every 1,000 by a *naqīb alf*, and
in the case of war every forty of them were commanded by
a *muqaddam al-ḥalqa*.[4] Among the royal mamlūks we
must note (a) *al-khāṣṣikiyya*, viz. personal aides-de-camp and
messengers of the sultan,[5] and (b) *muqaddamū l-mamālīk*,
the eunuchs who were military instructors of the young
mamlūks. During the years of their military education the
mamlūks were considered as temporary slaves and denoted
as *al-mamālīk al-kitābiyya*, having a much higher social
position than the black and native slaves (*'abīd* and *ghilmān*),

---

[1] *Ṣubḥ*, iv, p. 14, l. 8, to p. 16, l. 11. *Ḍaw' al-Ṣubḥ*, i, p. 244, l. 18, to
p. 245, l. 18. *Nujūm*, vi, p. 386, l. 17, to p. 387, l. 9. *Ẓāhirī*, p. 113, ll. 4–18 ;
p. 116, ll. 7–19.

[2] *Khiṭaṭ*, ii, p. 217, ll. 20–3. Ẓāhirī, p. 116, l. 18. Ṣubḥ, iv, p. 16, ll. 9–11.
Ḍaw' al-Ṣubḥ, i, p. 245, ll. 16–17. Ibn Iyās, i, p. 331, ll. 3–5. There were
also divisions of *al-baḥriyya* in Syro-Palestinian provinces (*Ṣubḥ*, iv, p. 182,
on Damascus ; Ẓāhirī, p. 132, on al-Karak).

[3] Ẓāhirī, p. 115, ll. 17–20. On the term *qarānīṣ* (or *qarāniṣa*, sing. *qirnāṣ*),
cf. my notes in *RÉI.*, 1935, pp. 243–4. Their privileges dated only from
Sultan Barqūq.

[4] *Khiṭaṭ*, ii, p. 216, ll. 5–6 ; p. 218, ll. 8–9. Ẓāhirī, p. 116, l. 17. Ṣubḥ, iv,
p. 16, l. 7.

[5] Ẓāhirī, pp. 115–16 ; cf. Ibn Iyās, iv, p. 358, ll. 14–15. In the lists of
the Mamlūk army in 1315 the terms *khāṣṣikiyya* and *kharjiyya* designate
respectively senior and junior emirs of each grade (*Khiṭaṭ*, ii, p. 217, l. 37,
to p. 218, l. 5).

although being equal to them in legal respect. Those of the sultan were trained in the barracks (*ṭibāq*, sing. *ṭabaqa*) of the citadel of Cairo.[1] The title of "emir", employed by the Arabic-writing clerks as translation of "bey",[2] was accorded to every knight in official documents addressed to him, and there were some *ajnād al-ḥalqa* who had in their service 1–4 mamlūks[3]; however, the historiographers (excepting Ibn Yahyā) denote as emirs only those feudatories who had in their service not less than 5 mamlūks. An "emir of 100" had in his service 100 (and sometimes up to 120) mamlūks[4]; an "emir *al-ṭablakhāna*"[5]—40 (and sometimes up to 80); an "emir of 10"—10 (and sometimes 20); an "emir of 5" —5. In the case of war an "emir of 100" commanded also 1,000 *ajnād al-ḥalqa*; hence he was designated also as "emir of 100 and commander (*muqaddam*) of 1,000", merely "commander", and even "emir of 1,000" (especially by Ibn Iyās). As regards the royal mamlūks, being on duty they were also commanded by emirs, but the person of commander and his grade, as well as the number of royal mamlūks under his orders, were fixed separately for each case by the sultan,[6] whereas *ajnād al-ḥalqa* were distributed among the "commanders of 1,000" in a fixed manner.[7]

---

[1] *Ṣubḥ*, iii, p. 481, l. 18. *Ẓāhirī*, p. 27, ll. 5–7. *Ḥawādith*, p. 658, ll. 2–3. Some *muqaddamū l-mamālīk* served as superintendents of barracks, and were denoted as *aghawāt al-ṭibāq* (cf. Ibn Iyās, i, p. 168, l. 6; iv, p. 485); the remaining were entrusted only with instruction.

[2] Poliak in *RÉI.*, 1936, p. 264, n. 3.

[3] Id. in *RÉI.*, 1935, p. 247, n. 4.

[4] These private mamlūks were denoted as *mamālīk al-umarā'* (*Nujūm*, vi, p. 387), *jund* (or *ajnād*) *al-umarā'* (*Khiṭaṭ*, ii, p. 216; *Ṣubḥ*, vii, p. 159), *tawāshiyya* (*Ṣubḥ*, vii, p. 159; Ibn Yahyā, pp. 79, 93–4; Ibn al-Shiḥna, p. 225; not to be confounded with eunuchs, as Quatremère does in *Sulūk*, I, ii, p. 132), and *fawāris* (*Khiṭaṭ*, ii, p. 215; *Ṣubḥ*, iv, p. 15), the latter term being also applied to other knights.

[5] = Before whose house a military orchestra played several times every day, like before the house of an "emir of 100"; cf. *Sulūk*, I, i, pp. 173–4, n. 54; Ibn Iyās, v, p. 270, ll. 11–21.

[6] Ibn Iyās, iv, p. 51, ll. 6–7; p. 99, l. 8; p. 105, ll. 19–21; v, p. 126, ll. 19–21.

[7] *Khiṭaṭ*, i, p. 87, l. 39, to p. 88, l. 10. *Nujūm*, vi, p. 387, ll. 1–2.

In reward for the service (*khidma*), the royal mamlūks held fiefs and received a monthly pecuniary pay (*jāmakiyya*), an annual pecuniary allowance for the purchase of dresses (*kiswa*), regular allocations in kind (*rawātib*)—meat (daily), sheep before the feast of 'Īd al-Naḥr (*daḥāyā*), barley for horses, cloths for tents (*khām*)—and extraordinary pecuniary · grants (*nafaqa*) in the case of war, on the accession of a new sultan (*nafaqat al-bay'a*) or merely to make them more satisfied with the government.[1] In 1395 Sultan Barqūq transformed the fief of his late son (an " emir of 100 "), Muḥammad, into a royal domain, the revenues of which were devoted to the payment of *jāmakiyya* to the royal mamlūks. The department established for the administration of this domain, *dīwān* [*al-iqṭā'*] *al-mufrad* or *al-dīwān al-mufrad*, was managed by the royal major-domo, *al-ustādār al-kabīr* (hence it was denoted also as *dīwān al-ustādāriyya*). Afterwards this department was charged with additional duties (it had to supply *kiswa* and barley to the royal mamlūks, salary and barley to civil and religious officials of the sultan and to his commercial agents), and in order to meet the cost of these responsibilities it received new estates (former fiefs) and the right to levy money from Egyptian district governors and Bedouin <u>shaykhs</u> for their appointment.[2] For the supply of meat to the royal mamlūks the Egyptian vizier was responsible, and his department (*dīwān al-wizāra* or *dīwān al-dawla*) also had in its disposition particular sources of revenue : landed estates, specified taxes, mines of natron in al-Ṭarrāna.[3] The supply of *daḥāyā*, of munitions in the case of war, and sometimes of uniforms, was

---

[1] See, e.g. Ibn Iyās, ii, p. 57, ll. 20–1 ; p. 304, l. 21 ; iv, pp. 13–14, 177, 235, 369 ; Ṣubḥ, iv, p. 51, l. 8 ; *Nujūm*, vi, p. 387, ll. 5–6. " *Nafaqat al-salṭana* " (Ibn Iyās, i, p. 260, l. 10) = " *nafaqat al-bay'a* ".

[2] *Nujūm*, v, p. 626, ll. 6–13 ; vi, p. 104, l. 20 ; p. 493, ll. 12–14. *Manhal*, v, f. 109b. Ḥawādith, p. 38, l. 5 ; p. 691. Ẓāhirī, p. 106, ll. 21–2 ; p. 107, ll. 4–17. *Sulūk*, I, i, pp. 25–7, n. 25. Ṣubḥ, iii, p. 457, ll. 2–7 ; vi, p. 215, l. 6.

[3] Ḥawādith, pp. 253–4, 292, 321, 691. pp. 455–6.

among the duties of another royal office, the similarly organized *dīwān al-khāṣṣ*, established by Sultan Muḥammad b. Qalāūn and conducted by *nāẓir al-khāṣṣ*, with whose duties the vizier was formerly charged.[1] This division of the treasury into independent departments, each having its own revenues and responsible for particular items of the state budget, was caused by financial difficulties, but was unable to overcome them, although the managers of departments gradually became their farmers.

The knights of *al-ḥalqa* held fiefs, and prior to 1298 they and their servants received meals from the " emirs of 100 " to whom they were attached, *muḍāfūn*.[2] The emirs held fiefs, received *nafaqa* before going to war, and those of them who dwelt in Cairo received fixed allocations of meat, bread, spices, vegetable oil, and forage, and the most influential also dresses and wax.[3] Twice a year the sultan gave to the emirs of Cairo horses as gifts,[4] and the most influential of them often received allodial lands and houses.[5] In winter the royal mamlūks and the emirs of Cairo received, instead of barley, strips of the great royal pasturage in the neighbourhood of Giza, sown with clover and lucern-grass, and denoted in Arabic as *al-rabī'* and in Turkish as *otlāq* (in Arabized form *iṭlāq-āt*). The size of these strips varied from half a *faddān* [6] to hundreds of *faddāns*, according to the grade of each holder and to the number of his horses. The strips were redivided each year by the vizier.[7] Sometimes

---

[1] Ẓāhirī, pp. 108–9. Ṣubḥ, iii, p. 456.

[2] *Khiṭaṭ*, i, p. 87, l. 39, to p. 88, l. 2.

[3] Ṣubḥ, iv, p. 51, ll. 7–8. Ḍaw' al-Ṣubḥ, i, p. 258, ll. 15–16.

[4] *Khiṭaṭ*, ii, p. 216, ll. 29–30.

[5] Ṣubḥ, iv, p. 55, ll. 14–17.

[6] The Egyptian *faddān* was prior to Muḥammad 'Alī 5929 square metres, but he gradually reduced it to 4200,83, i.e. about an acre (see e.g. Jabartī, iv, p. 208, ll. 24 ff.; Prince Omar Toussoun, *Mémoire sur les finances de l'Égypte*, Cairo, 1924, pp. 115–19).

[7] *Sulūk*, i, i, pp. 16–17, n. 16. *Khiṭaṭ*, ii, p. 216, ll. 28–30. Ibn Iyās, i, pp. 137, 242 ; ii, pp. 54, 180, 247, 313, 314, 318 ; iv, pp. 283, 335, 482 ; v, pp. 266–7. Ṣubḥ, iii, p. 456, ll. 3–4. Nujūm, vi, pp. 251, 253. Ḥawādith, pp. 19, 94, 251, 462, 466, 537. Manhal, i, f. 21a.

a feudatory (as some other persons and institutions) received from the sultan a regular pecuniary present, *masmūḥ*.[1] The private mamlūks received no fiefs or allowances from the sultan, but each emir was obliged to divide two-thirds of the revenue of his fief among his mamlūks, by granting them either portions of his fief[2] or pecuniary allowances from its revenue.[3] He was, however, entitled to give them uneven shares,[4] and even, on condition of their explicit consent, to take for himself more than a third.[5] The emir paid them also portions of the *nafaqa* received by him.

The contingent of troops was not fixed. Some sources ascribe to prominent reigns great numbers of the royal mamlūks, e.g. about 16,000 under Baybars I, 12,000 (or 7,000) under Qalāūn, 12,000 under Khalīl, more than 12,000 *mushtarawāt* under Muḥammad b. Qalāūn[6]; it seems, however, that they never exceeded several thousands.[7] Under Muḥammad b. Qalāūn *al-khāṣṣikiyya* amounted to 40, under Barsbāy to 1,000, under al-Ghawrī to 1,200.[8] The total number of *muqaddamū l-mamālīk* amounted in 1315 to 40,[9] while that of *aghawāt al-ṭibāq* was probably equal to the number of barracks, viz. 12.[10] In the time of peace all the royal mamlūks were concentrated in Egypt (and accordingly only there we find lands allotted to *d. al-mufrad* and

---

[1] Sakhāwī, i, p. 61, l. 20 ; p. 63, ll. 19, 22. *Hawādith*, p. 253, ll. 11–14. *CIA.*, ii (A), *Syrie du Nord*, No. 44. Possibly identical with *mu'taddāt* in Ibn Iyās, iv, p. 43, ll. 15–16 ; p. 46, ll. 19–21.

[2] *Khiṭaṭ*, ii, p. 216, l. 2. Nuwayrī, viii, p. 207, ll. 1–5.

[3] Ibn Iyās, ii, p. 337, ll. 21–6. The third which remained to the emir was denoted as his *khāṣṣ* (Nuwayrī, viii, p. 207, ll. 3, 5 ; Ibn Yaḥyā, p. 92, l. 19, to p. 94, l. 10), or *khāṣṣa* (*Subḥ*, vi, p. 201, l. 19).

[4] *Khiṭaṭ*, ii, p. 216, l. 11.

[5] Ibid., l. 3.

[6] Ẓāhirī, p. 116, ll. 7–8. *Khiṭaṭ*, i, p. 95, ll. 5–6. Ibn Iyās, i, p. 173, l. 14.

[7] In 1315 there were 2,000 common mamlūks and 40 *muqaddams* ; about a hundred years later the total number of the royal mamlūks and of the Egyptian knights of *al-ḥalqa* was less than 5,000, and among them less than 1,000 were real warriors (*Khiṭaṭ*, i, p. 95, ll. 12–14 ; ii, p. 218, ll. 9–10).

[8] Ẓāhirī, p. 116, ll. 1–3. Ibn Iyās, v, p. 5, ll. 5–6.

[9] *Khiṭaṭ*, ii, p. 218, ll. 8–9.

[10] Ẓāhirī, p. 27, ll. 5–7.

d. al-wizāra) ; most of them dwelt in Cairo, where they hired private houses with stables.[1] As regards the emirs and the knights of *al-ḥalqa*, it must be remembered that the Mamlūk state was divided into several provinces (*mamālik*), which replaced the former Ayyūbid and Latin states, and that each province had its own emirs and knights, who dwelt for the most part in its administrative centre. The fief of an emir (or knight) was in the province where he served, and consequently on his transfer from one province to another he received a new fief.[2] Only in exceptional cases, when there were no vacant [3] fiefs in his new province, or as a special favour of the sultan, he retained his former fief.[4] The emirs were everywhere created directly by the sultan,[5] but the Syro-Palestinian knights of *al-ḥalqa* were recommended to the sultan by the governors-general of their respective provinces, and the governor-general's name was mentioned in their feudal charters.[6] In A.H. 815 and 875 the sultan accorded for a short time the right to dub emirs and knights in Syria and in Palestine, and to grant them fiefs, to the emir who commanded in chief the local troops (Nawrūz al-Ḥāfiẓī in the first case, Yashbak al-Dawādār in the second).[7] According to Ẓāhirī,[8] who indicates in general the greatest

[1] Ibn Iyās, iv, p. 369.

[2] *Ḥawādith*, p. 350, l. 12 ; p. 357, ll. 13–15 ; p. 372, l. 19 ; p. 662, l. 6. *Nujūm*, vi, p. 314, l. 5.

[3] The vacant fief is denoted as *shāghir* (*Nujūm*, vii, p. 851, l. 12), *maḥlūl* (*Khiṭaṭ*, ii, p. 217, l. 15), *mutawaffir* (Ibn Iyās, ii, p. 277), *muwaffar* (*Nujūm*, vi, p. 68, l. 17), and *mu'akhkhar* (*Nujūm*, vi, p. 7, l. 14).

[4] A. F., i v, p. 61, l. 29 ; p. 71, ll. 26–7 ; p. 74, ll. 6–8. *Manhal*, iii, f. 36a l. 11 ; f. 48b, l. 1. Ibn Iyās, iv, p. 125, l. 21.

[5] *Ṣubḥ*, iv, p. 50, l. 16, to p. 51, l. 2. *Khiṭaṭ*, ii, p. 217, ll. 24–6.

[6] *Ṣubḥ*, iv, p. 51, ll. 3–6 ; p. 184, ll. 13–15 ; p. 217, ll. 6–7 ; xii, p. 21, ll. 16–17 ; p. 218, l. 19.

[7] Ibn Iyās, i, p. 358, l. 8 ; ii, p. 127, ll. 2–7. *Nujūm*, vi, p. 314, l. 1.

[8] pp. 104, 131–5. Sometimes it is not clear whether he includes those emirs who held administrative dignities in general figures, and then we have decided according to the relative significance of the province in question. According to *Ṣubḥ*, iv, p. 182, ll. 16–20, there were in the province of Damascus up to ten " emirs of 100 ", 40–150 emirs *al-ṭabl.*, 2,150 (!) "   of 10 ". The governors-general were as a rule " emirs of 100 ".

figures which were ever attained, there were in the province of Damascus (= South Syria, most of the Lebanon, Northern Trans-Jordan, Samaria and Northern Judæa) 12 " emirs of 100 ", 20 *al-ṭabl.*, 60 lower emirs, 12,000 knights of *al-ḥalqa* ; in the province of Ṣafad (= Galilee) 3 *al-ṭabl.*, about 20 lower emirs, 1,000 knights of *al-ḥalqa* ; in that of Gaza (= the south-western corner of Palestine) 2 emirs *al-ṭabl.*, 1,000 knights of *al-ḥalqa* ; in that of Tripoli (= the region of Tripoli and the modern land of the 'Alawīs) 4 " emirs of 100 ", 10 emirs *al-ṭabl.*, about 30 lower emirs, 3–4,000 knights of *al-ḥalqa* ; in that of Ḥamā 4 emirs *al-ṭabl.*, more than 20 lower emirs, about 3–4,000 knights of *al-ḥalqa* ; in that of Aleppo 6–9 " emirs of 100 ", 10 emirs *al-ṭabl.*, 20 lower emirs, 6,000 knights of *al-ḥalqa* ; in that of Malaṭya 8 emirs *al-ṭabl.*, more than 30 lower emirs, 1,000 knights of *al-ḥalqa* ; on the province of al-Karak (= Southern Trans-Jordan) he supplies no detailed data. *Muqṣid* [1] attributes to the province of Damascus 8 " emirs of 100 ", 21 *al-ṭabl.*, 22 " emirs of 20 ", 51 " emirs of 10 ", 23 " emirs of 5 ", and to that of Ṣafad 4 *al-ṭabl.*, 3 " emirs of 20 ", 6 " emirs of 10 ", 3 " emirs of 5 ". The whole of Egypt was from the military standpoint a single province, where the local knights of *al-ḥalqa* were dubbed directly by the sultan. Sometimes there was, however, the post of vice-sultan, who could grant small fiefs (the annual revenue of which was less than 400 or 600 *dīnārs jayshī*) without consulting the sultan.[2] Under the first Mamlūk sultans there were in Egypt 24 " emirs of 100 " ; after the foundation of *d. al-mufrad* their number sunk to 18–20 (because some vacant fiefs of them became its domains) ; under Sultan Khushqadam to 13 ; under Jaqmaq to 11 ; in A.H. 908 it was again 24, and in A.H. 920 it rose to 27.[3] The number of lower emirs was constantly shifting.[4] In 1315 the total figure

---

[1] Cited by Gaudefroy-Demombynes, pp. 142, 234.

[2] Ibn Iyās, i, p. 229, ll. 2–4. *Sulūk*, I, ii, p. 95, n. 113.

[3] *Ṣubḥ*, iv, p. 14, ll. 13–18. *Ḥawādith*, p. 452, l. 21. *Nujūm*, vii, p. 237, l. 13. Ibn Iyās, iv, p. 30, l. 14 ; p. 358, l. 6 ; p. 434, l. 7.

[4] *Ṣubḥ*, iv, p. 15. *Ḍaw' al-Ṣubḥ*, i, 245.

of Egyptian emirs *al-ṭabl.* and " emirs of 10 " was 491, and in 1516 it amounted to more than 300, which was an increase in comparison with the immediately preceding period.[1] In 1315 there were in Egypt 8,932 knights (and 204 officers) of *al-ḥalqa*, whereas in 1418 those who dwelt in Cairo (= the majority) were scarcely more than 400.[2] In consequence, the real number of knights of *al-ḥalqa* who were commanded by an " emir of 100 " was as a rule much less than the nominal thousand. ·

There were also auxiliary troops of natives : (*a*) Turcoman and Kurdish shepherd tribes, employed by the Mamlūks as military colonists in all parts of Syria, Palestine and the Lebanon.[3] In 1267 Baybars I settled Turcomans in the Palestinian maritime plain as guardians against the invasions of Crusaders,[4] and in 1306 the region of Kasrawān (in the North Lebanon) was divided into fiefs among 300 Turcoman knights, who had to watch shores and routes from Anṭalyās (near Beirut) to the boundary of the province of Tripoli.[5] Influential tribal chieftains had the grade of emirs (of 10, 20, and *al-ṭabl.*), but they were not equal to the " Turkish " emirs of the same grades, the distinction being emphasized by the external form of their feudal charters.[6] (*b*) Bedouin tribes, the chieftains of which held fiefs on the condition of guarding roads and punishing highwaymen,[7] sending horses

---

[1] *Khiṭaṭ*, ii, p. 217, l. 37, to p. 218, l. 6. Ibn Iyās, v, p. 5, ll. 8–9.

[2] *Khiṭaṭ*, ii, p. 218, ll. 8–11. *Nujūm*, vi, pp. 388–9. The figure 24,000 (*Khiṭaṭ*, i, p. 95, l. 11 ; Ẓāhirī, pp. 104, 116), is based upon the supposition that the number of thousands of these knights should be equal to the number of " emirs of 100 ", and upon the confusion with the total contingent of the Egyptian army in 1315 (*Khiṭaṭ*, ii, p. 217, l. 35).

[3] Ẓāhirī, p. 105. *Ṣubḥ*, iii, p. 182 ; vii, pp. 190, 282 ; xii, p. 218. *Nujūm*, vi, p. 364. Ibn al-Shiḥna, pp. 228, 264. Ibn Yaḥyā, pp. 107, 182.

[4] *Sulūk*, I, ii, p. 51. Cf. *Ṣubḥ*, xii, p. 218, l. 16.

[5] Ibn Yaḥyā, pp. 33, 37, 42, 169. Cf. Shidyāq, pp. 212, 346.

[6] *Ṣubḥ*, vii, p. 190, ll. 6–7, 17 ; xiii, p. 158, l. 19 ; p. 198, ll. 10–11.

[7] Ibn Khaldūn, v, p. 383, ll. 15–16 ; vi, p. 6, ll. 2–3, 9, 22 ; p. 9, l. 12. *Ṣubḥ*, iii, p. 458, l. 4. *Sulūk*, I, i, pp. 169–170. Every chieftain was responsible for a specified territorial division (*darak*), and his watchmen (*khufarā'*) camped there in their tents on roads : *Ṣubḥ*, xiii, p. 95, ll. 14–19. *Nujūm*, vi, p. 292, l. 3 ; p. 481, l. 8.

as annual gifts to the sultan,[1] and supplying in the case of emergency an auxiliary cavalry.[2] The chieftains of al-Sharqiyya and of the Sinaitic desert had an additional duty, to supply post-horses for the lines Bilbays–Damietta and Bilbays–al-Kharrūba (the latter being a portion of the line Cairo–Damascus).[3] A humbler chieftain (*shaykh al-'arab*) was reckoned a knight of *al-ḥalqa*,[4] a more influential had the title of emir, without being equal to a " Turkish " emir. A quite exceptional position was held by the chief emir of Āl [5] Faḍl (the family which dominated the northern Syrian desert, possible ancestors or kinsmen of the tribe of the same name which roams to-day to the east of the Lake Tiberias), denoted as " the king of the bedouins " or " the emir of the desert ".[6] Sometimes, not being content with their Syrian fiefs, Āl Faḍl passed for some time to the side of the Iranian Mongols, and the fiefs granted to them in such cases by the Mongols contained almost the whole of Iraq.[7] The chief emir granted fiefs to those bedouins who were in his service,[8]

---

[1] *Ta'rīf*, p. 110, ll. 14–15. Ṣubḥ, xii, p. 127, ll. 15–17 ; p. 135, ll. 1–2.

[2] *Nujūm*, vi, p. 71, l. 15, to p. 72, l. 4. Ibn Khaldūn, p. 6, l. 9. Ibn Iyās, i, p. 331, ll. 7–10.

[3] Ṣubḥ, iii, p. 458, l. 4 ; xiv, p. 377, ll. 1–3.

[4] Ṣubḥ, iii, p. 458, ll. 3–4.

[5] The family names of aristocratic families were very seldom derived, as in Europe, from the locality of the hereditary fief (e.g. the family al-Shārinqāshī in Egypt in the fifteenth century : Sakhāwī, viii, p. 203, l. 23)· The foreign-born knights called themselves after their former masters : *under the Mamlūks* : Jakam *min* 'Awaḍ or Jakam al-'Awaḍī = Jakam, a freedman of 'Awaḍ ; *under the Ottomans* : Murād-bey Muḥammad = the bey Murād, a freedman of Muḥammad. The family names of natives (and *awlād al-nās*) were for the most part personal names or nicknames of their ancestors, preceded under the Mamlūks by *ibn* (in the singular), *banū, awlād*, or *āl* (in the plural), and under the Ottomans employed according to the following examples : (*a*) sing. : X. Shihāb = X. al-Shihābī, plur. : *Banū* (or *Āl, Bayt*) Shihāb = al-Shihābiyyūn = al-Shihābiyya ; (*b*) sing. : X. al-Khāzin, plur. : al-Khawāzina = *Banū* (or *Āl, Bayt*) al-Khāzin.

[6] " *Malik al-'arab*," " *amīr al-malā*' " : *Nujūm*, vi, p. 283, l. 18 ; p. 800, l. 12.

[7] *Sulūk*, i, ii, p. 17. A. F., iv, p. 73, l. 19 ; p. 85, l. 28. Ibn Ḥajar, iv, p. 370, l. 9. Ibn Baṭṭūṭa, i, p. 171, l. 2.

[8] *Ta'rīf*, p. 110, l. 4 (possibly they were reckoned his mamlūks).

but there were also some other members of his family who received from the sultan the title of emir and fiefs.[1] Āl ʿAlī (a branch of Āl Faḍl, roaming in the plain of Damascus), Āl Murrā (or Mirā, Mirāʾ, in the Hauran) and Banū ʿUqba (in Moab) had also respectively a chief emir and several subordinate emirs; B. Mahdī (in Gilead) 1-4 emirs; sometimes the higher chieftains of Jarm (in the province of Gaza), Zubayd, and al-Mashāriqa (scattered in Syria), were also dubbed emirs.[2] In Egypt there were at the commencement of the Mamlūk epoch, according to al-Ḥamdānī, at least 12 bedouin dynasties of emirs (5 in the south, 7 in al-Sharqiyya), but none of them retained its influence until the end of this epoch.[3] The emigration of the Hawwāra tribe from al-Buḥayra to Upper Egypt in the fourteenth century brought to their chieftains, B. ʿUmar, the dignity of emirs.[4] Other families of bedouin emirs in Egypt towards the end of the Mamlūk epoch were: B. al-Aḥdab[5] in Upper Egypt, B. Baqar[6] in al-Sharqiyya, B. Baghdād[7] in al-Gharbiyya, B. Murʿā[8] in al-Buḥayra. (c) Syro-Palestinian and Lebanese tribes of cultivators, designated as al-ʿashīr, al-ʿushrān, or al-ʿashāʾir.[9] In the case of war the government hired the tribesmen as mercenary footmen, armed with arrows and stones. We hear in this connection especially on (1) tribesmen of Samarian

---

[1] Ibid., p. 79, l. 15, to p. 80, l. 1. A. F., iv, p. 81, ll. 1-2; p. 91, ll. 17-18; p. 148, l. 31.

[2] Cf. the lists of Syro-Palestinian bedouin tribes in Taʿrīf, pp. 79-80; Ṣubḥ, iv, pp. 203-215, 231-2, 242-3; vii, pp. 184-9; Ibn Khaldūn, vi, pp. 6-11. Muqṣid, cited by Gaudefroy-Demombynes, p. 200, n. 1. Ẓāhirī, 2, l. 13; p. 136, l. 6.

[3] Cf. the detailed lists in Taʿrīf, pp. 76-7; Ṣubḥ, iv, 67-72; vii, pp. 160-2.

[4] Ṣubḥ (the aforementioned lists). Ibn Iyās, ii, pp. 96, 166, 171, 180-2, 229, 233, 240, 248, 279, etc.

[5] Mentioned in A.H. 754 as chieftains of the ʿArak tribe (Ibn Iyās, i, p. 200), in A.H. 928 as chieftains of Hawwāra (ibid., v, pp. 429, 431).

[6] Ibn Iyās, i, p. 331; ii, pp. 127, 197; v, pp. 108, 235, etc. Of the Judhām tribe.

[7] Ibn Iyās, ii, p. 105; v, p. 431.

[8] Many times in the vols. iv-v of Ibn Iyās.

This appellation is treated by me in RÉI., 1934, pp. 264-5.

hills,[1] who were denoted also as " bedouins " (*'urbān*), but
are not mentioned in the lists of genuine bedouin tribes, and
on (2) Lebanese tribesmen,[2] but also on those of the provinces
of Tripoli, Ṣafad, and Aleppo.[3] Sometimes they were also
hired as horsemen: according to Ẓāhirī [4] *al-'ashīr* were
headed by 35 chieftains (*muqaddamūn*), who could mobilize
up to 35,000 horsemen, while 180,000 could be supplied by
the Turcomans, more than 20,000 by the Kurds, and 93,000
by the bedouins (29,000 Syro-Palestinian, 33,000 Egyptian,
31,000 of the Hijaz and Mesopotamia). The most important families of chieftains were (1) B. Ṣubḥ (or Ṣubayḥ)
the foremost Lebanese chieftains under the first Mamlūk
sultans [5]; (2) B. Bishāra, the most important chieftains of
al-'ashīr in the fourteenth and fifteenth centuries, the centre
of whose activities seems to be that Shī'ite region which
forms now, under the name of Bilād Bishāra, the southern
part of the Lebanese Republic [6]; (3) B. al-Ḥanash, in the
al-Biqā' plain and in the neighbourhood of Ḥamā, destroyed
at the time of the Ottoman conquest (the survivors were
exterminated in 1541) [7]; (4) B. al-Ḥamrā' in the plain of
al-Biqā', fief-holders in the fourteenth and fifteenth
centuries [8]; (5) B. Buḥtur, denoted also as Āl Tanūkh,
chieftains of the al-Gharb region near Beirut, fief-holders
since 1147,[9] who retained their influence after the Ottoman

---

[1] Ibn Iyās, i, pp. 281, 292, 329, 342, 353 ; ii, pp. 109, 123, 250, 252 ;
iv, pp. 408, 448 ; v, pp. 88, 239, 377. Mujīr, pp. 666, 673, 675–6. *Ḥawādith*,
pp. 701, 709.

[2] Ibn Yaḥyā, pp. 105–6.

[3] Ibn al-Shiḥna, p. 264, l. 4. *Nujūm*, vi, p. 49, ll. 5–6 ; p. 94, l. 11.
Cf. *Ṣubḥ*, xii, p. 109, l. 6 (on Ḥimṣ).

[4] p. 105, ll. 16–17. Cf. Ibn Iyās, p. 331, l. 10.

[5] Ibn Yaḥyā, pp. 33, 34, 84, 96, 105, 136. Anonym, pp. 140, 144. *Taqwīm*,
p. 40, n. 1. *Manhal*, iv, f. 68b. Shidyāq, pp. 48, 49, 250.

[6] *Nujūm*, vi, pp. 114, 778. *Ḥawādith*, pp. 56, 109. Ibn Iyās, ii, p. 238.
Sakhāwī, iii, p. 138. Ibn Ṭūlūn, *Rasā'il Ta'rīkhiyya* (Damascus, A.H. 1348),
iv, p. 60. In A.H. 824 they founded a new town on the site of Tyre.

[7] Ibn Yaḥyā, p. 198. Ibn Iyās, v, pp. 104, 105, 114, 248. Rustem,
pp. 55–6. Shidyāq, pp. 246, 251, 348.

[8] Ibn Yaḥyā, pp. 111, 154, 184, 225–6, 231. Shidyāq, pp. 155b, 243.

[9] Ibn Yaḥyā, p. 45, ll. 7 ff. Ibn Ḥajar, ii, pp. 54–5, No. 1586. Shidyāq,
p. 224, l. 18 ff.

conquest and were exterminated in 1633 ; (6) the Ramṭūnī chieftains in the same region, fief-holders since 1309, regarded by the dynasty of B. Ma'n in the seventeenth century as their ancestors [1] ; (7) B. Abī l-Jaysh of the same region, enemies of B. Buḥtur,[2] claimed by the modern Arslān emirs as their ancestors [3] ; (8) B. Ismā'īl and (9) B. 'Abd al-Qādir, who disputed under the Circassian sultans the dignity of the supreme *shaykh* of the Samarian tribes, *shaykh* ['urbān] *jabal Nābulus* [4] ; (10) as regard the claim of the Shihāb emirs, chieftains of Wādī l-Taym under the Ottoman rule (and chief emirs of the Lebanon between 1697–1841), that they held this chieftainship since Saladin,[5] the Mamlūk sources contain too little information on this region, so that we are not able to accept or to reject it. B. al-Ḥanash, B. al-Ḥamrā', B. Ismā'īl, and B. 'Abd al-Qādir were semi-bedouins ; B. Bishāra and B. Ṣubḥ probably Shī'ites [6] ; chieftains of al-Gharb outwardly Sunnis, in reality Druses.[7] Most of them were reckoned knights of *al-ḥalqa* and low emirs, the grade of emir *al-ṭabl.* being accorded only as an exceptional favour

---

[1] Poliak in *RÉI.*, 1935, p. 247, n. 6. Ibn Yaḥyā, pp. 158–165. *Manhal*, iii, f. 8a. Ibn Ḥajar, i, pp. 540–1, No. 1462. The tradition on the descent of B. Ma'n from a bedouin emir, Ma'n, who allegedly settled in the Lebanon in 1120 (Shidyāq, pp. 162b, 247), is a late fable, just as that upon their descent from Crusaders (in European sources). Ibn Yaḥyā does not know at all those members of this family who lived in the Mamlūk epoch according to Shidyāq, and the chieftains of al-Shūf were then not B. Ma'n (as alleged by Shidyāq) but B. Mi'ṣād (Ibn Yaḥyā, p. 173, l. 5). It seems from Shidyāq, p. 114, that after the Ramṭūnī pedigree had been abandoned by B. Ma'n, it was claimed by the family of 'Alam al-Dīn (who exterminated B. Buḥtur in 1633 and were exterminated in their turn in 1709) ; they, however, not only introduced in it some confusion and could not establish a continuous line of names since that time, but alleged that the first Ramṭūnī emir ('Alam al-Dīn) was a member of B. Buḥtur and seceded from them in 1301.

[2] Ibn Yaḥyā, pp. 47, 59, 69, 72–3, 81–2, 94, 97, 98, 99, 133, 180, 185, 190, 200.

[3] Shidyāq, pp. 668–675.

[4] *Ḥawādith*, p. 215. Ibn Iyās, ii, pp. 221, 234, 278. Mujīr, pp. 666, 669, 675. Sakhāwī, i, p. 10 ; viii, p. 70, No. 129.

[5] Shidyāq, pp. 44 ff.

[6] Cf. *Ṣubḥ*, iv, p. 153, l. 13 ; p. 154, l. 14.

Cf. Ibn Yaḥyā, p. 47, ll. 2–5 and n. 2 ; p. 158, l. 11 ;

to individuals. (*d*) Ismāʿīlīs, whose territory contained the castles Maṣyāf, al-Ruṣāfa, al-Khawābī, al-Qadmūs, al-Kahf, al-Manīqa, and al-ʿUllayqa (in the modern land of the ʿAlawīs). In 1269 this country (except Maṣyāf) became the fief of the Ismāʿīlī chief, Mubārak b. Riḍāʾ, dubbed *amīr al-ṭablakhāna*.[1] In 1271 it was completely annexed to the Mamlūk state, and the chieftains acquired a quite particular status : their duty was to send courageous terrorists against the sultan's enemies, they had no fiefs but received allowances from the revenue of these castles, and they were denoted in official letters not as emirs but as *atābaks*.[2]

There were also small native auxiliary forces which were not organized on the tribal principle, and are not mentioned among the fief-holders : *balāṣiyya* and *ghilmān sulṭāniyya*.[3] In the fleet the sailors were considered as workers, whose duty was to build, repair, and conduct ships, whereas the warriors (*ghuzāt*) consisted of mamlūks and auxiliary troops. Shortly before the last Mamlūk-Ottoman war, Sultan al-Ghawrī hired an Ottoman admiral, Salmān, and his 2,000 seamen to conduct the war against the Portuguese on the Red Sea.[4] The same sultan established the corps of mercenary musketeers and artillerymen, *al-ṭabaqa al-khāmisa*,[5] which consisted of *awlād al-nās*,[6] Turcomans, Persians, etc.

The feudal aristocracy had considerable privileges. The lawsuits relating to the knights and emirs and to their fiefs were settled not by the *qāḍīs* and according to the Islamic law, but by the military judges (*ḥujjāb*) and according to the *siyāsa*, laws based upon the rules ("the Great Yāsa") of

---

[1] *Sulūk*, i, ii, p. 80.

[2] Ibn al-Shiḥna, p. 265. *Ṣubḥ*, iv, p. 146 ; vii, p. 228.

[3] e.g. Ibn Iyās, ii, p. 180 ; *Ḥawādith*, p. 190 ; Ẓāhirī, p. 132.

[4] Ibn Iyās, iv, pp. 365, 459 ; v, p. 199. He returned when Egypt was already Ottoman.

[5] Ibn Iyās, iv, pp. 206, 259, 269, 331, 360, 369, 436, etc.

[6] = " Persons of noble birth " : the natives descended from " Turkish " ancestors (and particularly the descendants of emirs). On their identity with *banū l-atrāk*, cf. Ibn Iyās, iv, p. 136, ll. 5, 8, 16.

Chingiz Khān.[1] Only the members of military class had coats of arms,[2] and they strove to make horse riding their exclusive prerogative.[3] Their turban (*taḥfīfa*) was distinct from that of the natives (*'imāma*), and only those of them who held fiefs directly from the sultan were entitled to gilded spurs and to embroideries (*ṭirāz*) on their sleeves.[4] Many offices (*al-wazā'if al-jayshiyya*), not necessarily of military character, were reserved for knights and emirs only ; but we often find " men of the sword " entrusted even with offices which had to be assigned, according to custom, to native religious and civil officials (*al-wazā'if al-dīniyya* and *al-wazā'if al-dīwāniyya*).[5] The qualities which the accomplished knight had to possess, *furūsiyya*, are to be defined rather as " physical culture " than as " chivalry " : among their " branches " (*anwā'* or *funūn al-furūsiyya*) we find [6] the correct use of bridle and spurs, the knowledge of pedigrees of horses, races, wrestling, lance exercises, the preparation of bows and arrows and their use, etc. The order of knights devoted to Muḥammad's posterity, *al-futuwwa*, which was headed by the sultan and open to native knights,[7] ceased to exist in the fourteenth century, probably owing to the growing exclusiveness of the " Turkish " nobility.

---

[1] Cf. the sources enumerated by me in *RÉI.*, 1935, pp. 235–6. Al-Ghawrī temporarily suspended the military courts of justice in A.H. 910 and 919 (Ibn Iyās, iv, pp. 77, 302, 312, 318, 320), but the final blow was given by the Ottoman conquest. The bedouins had their own *ḥujjāb* (A. F., iv, p. 113, ll. 12–13 ; *Manhal*, iv, f. 198a, l. 19), who probably decided according to tribal custom.

[2] Mayer, p. 3. This question is further elucidated by the same author in his article in *Syria*, xviii, 1937, pp. 389–393.

[3] *Ḥawādith*, pp. 76, 77, 91, 534, 538.

[4] *Khiṭaṭ*, ii, p. 217, ll. 11–12.

[5] e.g. the superintendent of waqfs (*nāẓir al-awqāf*) was often an emir, although this dignity was among *al-wazā'if al-dīniyya* ; cf. Ẓāhirī, p. 115, ll. 12–13 ; *Ḍaw' al-Ṣubḥ*, i, p. 251, ll. 3–5 ; *Manhal*, iv, f. 179b.

[6] Sakhāwī, iii, p. 41, ll. 10–11 ; p. 308, ll. 25–6 ; vi, p. 228, ll. 15–16. *Ḥawādith*, p. 585, ll. 1–2. Cf. the expression *'ilm al-furūsiyya* (Ibn Iyās, ii, p. 87, l. 22).

[7] *Sulūk*, i, i, p. 58, 163, 212, 223. Ibn 'Abd al-Ẓāhir, pp. 64 ff.

There remained in Syria and in Palestine, after their conquest by the Mamlūks in 1260, Latin enclaves (until 1291), Ayyūbid enclaves (al-Karak until 1263, Ḥimṣ until 1264, Ṣahyūn until 1271, Ḥamā until 1341), and two native states : the Druse Kasrawān (until 1300) and the Nuṣayrī ‘Amal al-Ẓinniyyīn (until 1306).[1]. Whereas the Latin and native enclaves were independent of the Mamlūk state,[2] the Ayyūbid were its feudatories. The Sultan of Ḥamā was entitled, according to the patent of 1313, to maintain 500 knights in his service, and consulted the Mamlūk sultan whenever he wished to create an emir.[3] Sometimes there were in al-Karak and in Ṣahyūn feudatory rulers of mamlūk stock, denoted respectively as Sultans and emirs[4] ; but in general the Mamlūks regarded Syria, Palestine, and the Lebanon as integral parts of their state, and divided them into the usual fiefs,[5] whereas other countries captured by them (as

---

[1] Cf. Poliak in *RÉI.*, 1934, p. 265 ; 1936, pp. 264–5. These regions probably were loose confederations of tribal chieftains (cf. on Kasrawān the later traditions in Shidyāq, pp. 208–212, which exaggerate the part played then by the Maronites). After the conquest these chieftains received no fiefs in their own regions, but those of them who emigrated from Kasrawān to Tripoli were dubbed knights of *al-ḥalqa* (Ibn Yaḥyā, p. 32, l. 7 ; read *akhbāz* !).

[2] Two rebel chieftains succeeded in establishing for a short time independent states : the bedouin sultan Ḥiṣn al-Dīn b. Tha‘lab, ruler of Upper Egypt under Aybak, Quṭuz, and Baybars I (*Ta‘rīf*, p. 188, ll. 6–12 ; *Ṣubḥ*, iv, p. 68, ll. 1–9 ; *Sulūk*, i, i, pp. 40–2), and the Turcoman emir Fāris, ruler of North-West Syria between A.H. 806–8, who confirmed the fiefs of those Mamlūk knights who consented to serve him (*Manhal*, iv, ff. 205–6 ; Sakhāwī, vi, p. 163, No. 540).

[3] A. F., iv, p. 74, ll. 23–7. *Ṣubḥ*, iv, p. 237, ll. 13–16.

[4] The contingent of troops maintained in al-Karak by the local sultans was greater than the troops stationed there when it was a simple province of the Mamlūk state (cf. *Manhal*, v, f. 112a, on Sultan Baraka-Khān). In Ṣahyūn the emir Sunqur al-Ashqar was entitled between 1280–7 to maintain 600 knights (*Sulūk*, ii, i, pp. 30–1), and Baybars al-Jāshnikīr received in 1310 the right to maintain 100 (A. F., iv, p. 60, ll. 1–2, 30), but was arrested on his way thither.

[5] Among the emirs who received fiefs in the Palestinian maritime plain in 1264, we find Badr al-Dīn Muḥammad, a son of Berke-Khān b. Jūchī

Barca, Nubia, the Hijaz, the Yaman, Cyprus, Diyār Bakr) remained autonomous tributary states. The emir of Medina held a small fief in Egypt.[1]

(the ruler of the Golden Horde and the suzerain of the Mamlūk state) : *Sulūk*, ɪ, ii, p. 14 (cf. *RÉI.*, 1935, p. 233).

[1] Ibn al-Jī'ān, p. 133, l. 12 ; p. 144, l. 21. Ibn Ḥajar, iii, p. 150, l. 10.

II. The Mamlūk Fiefs

The Mamlūk fief, denoted as *iqṭā'*, *khubz*, or *mithal*,[1] was
a source of revenue, temporarily conceded by the state to
a knight or emir, and bringing an average yearly income
corresponding to his military grade. In consequence of the
agrarian character of the countries in question, most of the
fiefs were landed estates, but many of them were annual
allowances from the revenue of a tax, custom, or excise
levied by the central government ; mines or specified taxes,
customs and excises levied by the fief-holders in places which
belonged to the central government, etc.[2] Land being regarded
only as a source of revenue, the territorial fief was not an
expanse containing villages, forests, mountains, meadows,
and deserts, but it consisted as a rule only of lands bringing
a fixed income, viz. of cultivated lands which belonged to the
inhabited places enumerated in the feudal charter.[3] In the
Moslem world uncultivated lands were always considered

---

[1] Cf. my notes on these terms in *JRAS.*, 1937, p. 99. The term *iqṭā'*
was sometimes employed also for the domains of *d. al-mufrad* and
d. al-dawla (*Hawādith*, pp. 253, 292, 321, 413), possibly because most of
their revenue was distributed among the knights. The same may be said
on the designation *aqāṭī' sulṭāniyya* for the crown domains in Egypt
after the Ottoman conquest (cf. Ibn Iyās, v, p. 420, ll. 8, 20, and
pp. 403–5). The domains held by the sultan for his private expenses are
never referred to as *iqṭā'*.

[2] Cf. the cases cited by me in *JRAS.*, 1937, pp. 101–2. The extraction
of salt from the river Nahr al-Dhahab was a portion of the fief of the
governor-general of Aleppo (Ibn al-Shiḥna, p. 47, ll. 14–15).

[3] The Egyptian forests were held by the sultan (*Khiṭaṭ*, i, p. 110, ll. 30–1,
37, to p. 111, l. 10), most of the Lebanese and Syro-Palestinian utilized
by the neighbours without restraint (Dimishqī, p. 199, ll. 13 ff. ; Ibn
al-Shiḥna, p. 127, l. 12). The hunting of birds was monopolized in Egypt
by the sultan's court (Ẓāhirī, p. 115, l. 4 ; pp. 127–8 ; *Ṣubḥ*, iv, p. 22,
ll. 14–16). The sultan had also habitual hunting grounds in the Libyan
desert, between the Pyramids and al-Ḥamāmāt in al-Buḥayra (A. F., iv,
pp. 30, 31, 93 ; *Ṣubḥ*, xiv, pp. 166–171 ; *Manhal*, iii, f. 64a ; f. 148a),
and the Syro-Palestinian governors-general had theirs in uncultivated
regions (*Ṣubḥ*, iv, p. 217, ll. 9–13) ; but these hunting grounds were not
a part of their *iqṭā'*, and were utilized only during a specified season.

as unowned, the right of pasturage on them [1] being accorded
to all herd-owners. On the other hand, although the
sultan sometimes delimited the grazing grounds of bedouin
and Turcoman tribes,[2] it was only a means to avoid feuds
among them, and in general it did not give them any additional
rights in these regions : e.g. the habitual encampments of
Āl Faḍl in the desert were not included in their fiefs,[3] which
consisted only of cultivated lands, villages, and towns. Moreover the villages and towns of which a fief consisted were
not necessarily adjacent or neighbouring ; on the contrary,
a Syrian, Palestinian, or Lebanese fief was, after 1313, scattered
as a rule in various parts of that province in which the knight
served, and an Egyptian, after 1315, in various parts of Egypt.
In Egypt a territorial fief of an emir usually contained 1–10
villages ; of a royal mamlūk—sometimes a village, more
often only half a village or less ; of a knight of *al-ḥalqa*—
only a portion of a village.[4] Since 1313–15 the sultan often
granted portions of different villages instead of a whole
village, and small portions of several scattered villages
instead of a great portion of a single village.[5] As we
have sought to prove in *JRAS.*, 1937, pp. 104–6, the
arable lands being annually redivided among the peasant
clans of which the village community consisted, and each
clan being entitled to a fixed share of the common arable,
the distribution of a single village among several feudatories
meant in practice that each of them was the lord of a particular

---

[1] And on the cultivable lands of villages after the harvest, cf. *Ṣubḥ*, vii,
p. 203, ll. 16 ff., and the Ottoman Land Code of 1858, art. 125. In Egypt,
however, the Mamlūk fief-holders levied taxes on herds pastured on those
lands which officially belonged to the villages held by them.

[2] *Sulūk*, ii, i, p. 23. *Nujūm*, vi, p. 340, l. 7. The Kurdish tribes are less
frequently mentioned by the sources because of their smaller number ;
most of them immigrated to Syria only after 1258 (*Sulūk*, i, i, pp. 79–80,
83 ; *Ta‘rīf*, p. 111, ll. 10–11).

[3] A. F., iv, p. 73, ll. 18–24 ; p. 81, l. 1.

[4] *Ṣubḥ*, iii, p. 457, l. 15, to p. 458, l. 2.

[5] *Khiṭaṭ*, i, p. 90, ll. 6–8 = *Manhal*, v, f. 96a, ll. 19–20.
ll. 4–5.

clan. The towns conceded as fiefs were then scarcely more than large villages ; we may mention among them Sarmīn,[1] Ma'arrat al-Nu'mān [2] and Salamiya [3] in North Syria ; Nablus [4] in Palestine ; Ushmūn,[5] Damanhūr,[6] Aṭfīḥ,[7] Aswān, and 'Aydhāb [8] in Egypt. Really great cities (as Cairo, Damascus, Aleppo), where the majority of emirs and knights dwelt, were divided into small allodial ground-plots, and their affairs were managed by the sultan or his local representative (= the governor-general).

The grant and supervision of fiefs were committed to the government department denoted as *dīwān al-jaysh* or *d. al-iqtā'*.[9] The central office in Cairo was divided into two principal sections : *d. al-jaysh al-miṣrī*, devoted to Egypt, and *d. al-jaysh al-shāmī*, devoted to Syria, Palestine, and the Lebanon.[10] Each of them was managed by a clerk denoted as *mustawfī* (sometimes also *mutawallī*, *ṣāhib*, or *kātib*) of the respective section.[11] Two humbler *mustawfīs* were entrusted

---

[1] Included in the fiefs of Āl Faḍl (A. F., iv, p. 73, l. 19 ; p. 120, l. 2 ; p. 142, l. 26 ; p. 144, l. 9). Centre of soap industry (Ibn Baṭṭūṭa, i, p. 145).

[2] Granted in A.H. 716 to the emir Muḥammad of Āl Faḍl (A. F., iv, p. 83, ll. 3–4).

[3] Included in the fiefs of Āl Faḍl since A.H. 658 : A. F., iii, p. 214, l. 26 ; Ibn Khaldūn, vi, p. 9, l. 9 ; *Ṣubḥ*, iv, p. 206, l. 7.

[4] At the end of the Ayyūbid domination and in the commencement of the Mamlūk it was usually divided between two " Turkish " emirs : *Sulūk*, I, i, p. 83 ; I, ii, pp. 172–3 ; *Manhal*, i, f. 5a.

[5] Sometimes granted as fief to some " emir of 100 " (Ibn al-Jī'ān, p. 46 ; Ibn Duqmāq, v, p. 69). Centre of the district al-Daqahliyya wa-l-Murtāḥiyya.

[6] Ibn al-Jī'ān, p. 116 ; Ibn Duqmāq, p. 101. Centre of the al-Buḥayra district.

[7] Ibn al-Jī'ān, p. 147. Centre of the al-Aṭfīḥiyya district.

[8] According to Ibn al-Jī'ān, in 1375 their lord was the governor-general of Upper Egypt, and in his own time the emir Yashbak al-Dawādār.

[9] *Ta'rīf*, p. 88, l. 18 ; p. 89, ll. 8–9. *Khiṭaṭ*, ii, p. 217, ll. 18, 28.

[10] Ẓāhirī, p. 103, ll. 15–19.

[11] *Sulūk*, I, i, pp. 202–5, n. 85. Ibn Iyās, iv, p. 35, ll. 5–6, 16 ; v, p. 4, ll. 8, 18. Sakhāwī, xi, p. 241, ll. 2–5. On the book-keeping of *d. al-jaysh*, see Nuwayrī, viii, pp. 200–13. Yaḥyā ibn al-Jī'ān, the *mustawfī* of Egypt in A.H. 882–5 (Ibn Iyās, ii, pp. 174, 196), gives in his *al-Tuhfa al-Saniyya* a detailed comparison of the distribution of Egyptian lands in 1375 and in his own time.

respectively with fiefs of the bedouins and with fiefs granted as pensions.[1] The chief manager, *nāẓir* [*dīwān*] *al-jaysh*, was responsible directly to the sultan, whereas his assistant, *ṣāḥib dīwān al-jaysh*, was a subordinate of the vice-sultan.[2] There were branches of *d. al-jaysh* in all centres of provinces.[3]

The revenue of fiefs was calculated by *d. al-jaysh* in a fictitious monetary unit, denoted as *dīnār jayshī*, which varied in 1315 from 10 to 7 dirhems (according to the fief-holder's grade), in 1375 had a uniform value of $13\frac{1}{3}$ dirhems, and afterwards lost all connection with the real monetary units, but was still employed to express the approximate proportion of revenues of various villages. We possess two lists of the *'ibra* (= the yearly average revenue, when expressed in *d.j.*) fixed for every description of Egyptian fiefs. One of them is from 1315, while the other, of more vague and elastic nature, seems to be the scale used throughout the Mamlūk epoch. We learn from them that the fief of an " emir of 100 " brought *ca.* 80–200,000 *d.j.* (in 1315 : 85–100,000) ; of an " emir *al-ṭabl. ca.* 23–30,000 (in 1315 : 15–40,000) ; of an " emir of 10 " from 9,000 and less (in 1315 : 5–10,000) ; of an " emir of 5 " 3,000 ; of a royal mamlūk (in 1315) 1,000–1,500 ; of a knight of *al-ḥalqa* from 250 and more (in 1315 : 300–1,000).[4] The *'ibra* included not all the revenues which were derived in reality by the fief-holder from his fief, but only those levied according to *al-sana al-jayshiyya* or *al-sana al-kharājiyya*,[5] the calendar year employed by *d. al-jaysh* in its calculations, which was identical with the Coptic solar year but was numbered according to that Moslem year in which it began. These revenues were denoted as

---

[1] *Sulūk*, loc. cit. The *mustawfī al-ṣuḥba*, who supervised the cadastral surveys, was not a clerk of *d. al-jaysh* but a subordinate of the vizier (*Ṣubḥ*, xi, p. 94 ; *Ḍaw' al-Ṣubḥ*, i, p. 251).

[2] *Ṣubḥ*, iv, p. 16, ll. 17–19 ; p. 17, ll. 13, 18–19.

[3] According to Ẓāhirī, p. 134, l. 8, also in Alexandria.

[4] I have compared these lists in a more detailed manner in *JRAS.*, 1937, pp. 99–103.

[5] *Ṣubḥ*, xiii, p. 97, l. 11. Ibn Iyās, i, p. 159, l. 9 ; iv, p. 392, l. 19.

al-māl al-kharājī,[1] while the taxes levied according to the lunar Moslem months were called *al-māl al-hilālī*.[2] The solar year being longer than the lunar by $\frac{1}{33}$, d. al-jaysh had to blot out in its accounts every 33rd *kharājī* year in order to adapt the dates of these years to those of the Moslem. In reality this operation (*taḥwīl al-sinīn*) was carried out only exceptionally,[3] so that during most of the Mamlūk epoch the feudatories could levy taxes from the peasants according to lunar years.[4] Sometimes the state obliged them (or their heirs) to transfer to the treasury the additional sums levied by them owing to the difference of the solar and lunar years, *al-tafāwut al-jayshī*.[5] This action took place after the feudatory's retirement, transfer to another province, or death, when the department called *d. al-sulṭān* or *d. al-murtaja'* (and managed by *mustawfī l-murtaja'*) had to decide whether he had levied, in his fief, taxes in advance for a longer period than that of his actual service.[6] The vacant fief was managed and exploited by the department designated as *dīwān al-dhakhīra* until its grant by the sultan to another feudatory.[7] The clerks of *d. al-jaysh* had to survey every three years the state of cultivation of feudal lands and the taxes actually levied by their holders.[8] In practice, however, as we see from the work of Ibn al-Jī'ān, the figures regarding

---

[1] Nuwayrī, viii, p. 245, ll. 8 ff. *Khiṭaṭ*, i, p. 103, ll. 22 ff. *Ṣubḥ*, iii, p. 452, ll. 14 ff.

[2] Nuwayrī, viii, pp. 228–233. *Khiṭaṭ*, i, p. 107, ll. 6–9. *Ṣubḥ*, iii, p. 471.

[3] Cf. the real cases (Ibn Iyās, i, p. 159, l. 9; Ibn Khaldūn, v, p. 410, ll. 7–10; *Ṣubḥ*, xiii, pp. 75–9), and the theoretic calculation in *Ṣubḥ*, xiii, p. 62, ll. 1–8.

[4] The primary purpose of the *taḥwīl* was to prevent such a levy: *Ṣubḥ*, xiii, p. 55, ll. 16 ff.

[5] Ibn Khaldūn, v, p. 410, l. 9. Nuwayrī, viii, p. 201, ll. 16 ff. Abū l-Fidā', iv, p. 149, ll. 11–14. *CIA.*, *Syrie du Nord*, No. 44 (misunderstood by Becker in *Der Islam*, i, p. 98).

[6] Nuwayrī, viii, p. 201, ll. 6 ff. *Khiṭaṭ*, ii, p. 217, ll. 29–31. *Ṣubḥ*, iv, p. 33, l. 16. Ẓāhirī, p. 110, ll. 4–7. *CIA.*, *Syrie du Nord*, No. 44. Sakhāwī, x, p. 289, ll. 14–18.

[7] Ibn Iyās, ii, p. 277, l. 16; p. 305, l. 8; iv, p. 14, l. 16. p. 418, l. 8; p. 452, ll. 18–20. Ẓāhirī, p. 110, ll. 3–4.

[8] Nuwayrī, viii, p. 297, ll. 7–13.

the extent of lands belonging to Egyptian villages and their
quality were copied until the end of the Mamlūk epoch from
the registers of the cadastral survey of 1315.[1] As regards
the *'ibra*, d. al-jaysh was able as a rule to record only the
cases of its diminution, because otherwise the feudatories
were unwilling to reveal the real condition of their fiefs,
fearing that the *'ibra*'s growth would induce the government
to diminish the fief's extent.[2]

The sultans struggled to make the fief-holders more and
more dependent on the central government. At the beginning
of the Mamlūk epoch we still find the influence of the Latin
and Ayyūbid feudal systems, which made the fief-holders
hereditary rulers of their respective regions.[3] The means
employed by the sultans to put an end to it was the *rawk*,
i.e. redistribution of lands between the sultan and the
feudatories. As I have suggested in another place,[4] the idea
was of Mongol origin, but the details of its execution were
copied from the annual redivisions of lands among the
members of the village community. A speedy cadastral
survey (*kashf al-bilād*) was made ; then the estates were
divided into royal and feudal; the feudal lands were
redivided into the necessary number of fiefs of various grades,
and the fiefs of each grade were distributed by a drawing of

---

[1] Cf. Ibn al-Jī'ān, p. 5, l. 16 ; p. 6, ll. 10–11 ; p. 39, l. 3 ; p. 99, l. 7 ;
p. 106, l. 25, etc. (note the exceptions in p. 139, ll. 1–2, 27).

[2] Cf. Ibn al-Jī'ān (especially p. 65, l. 16 ; p. 80, l. 17 ; p. 138, l. 11 ;
p. 160, l. 16) ; *Ṣubḥ*, iii, p. 442, ll. 12–20 ; *Ḍaw' al-Ṣubḥ*, i, p. 258, ll. 23 ff.

[3] On the Latin influence, cf. my notes in *JRAS.*, 1937, pp. 97–9.

[4] *RÉI.*, 1935, pp. 239–241. *Khiṭaṭ*, i, pp. 82–3, employs the term *rawk*
to denote the periodical redivisions of the state domains among tax-farmers
under the Fāṭimids, which were also preceded by cadastral surveys but
were not such faithful reproductions of the redistributions of common
lands in villages as the Mamlūk *rawks*. We find already under the
'Abbāsids the idea that the Kharājī lands and their revenues are a common
property of the Moslems in the same manner as the lands of a village are
a common property of the villagers (cf. the use of *fay'* in Abū Yūsuf's
Kitāb al-Kharāj, ed. Cairo A.H. 1346, p. 75, l. 19 ; p. 95, l. 20 ; p. 103, l. 2 ;
from p. 28, l. 2, we may deduce that such explications of this term as
are proposed by al-Māwardī and lexicographers are posterior inventions).

lots among the knights and emirs of that grade. There were three *rawks* : *al-rawk al-ḥusāmī* in Egypt in 1298 [1] ; *al-rawk al-nāṣirī* in Syria, Palestine, and the Lebanon in 1313 [2] ; *al-rawk al-nāṣirī* in Egypt in 1315. [3] Prior to the *rawks* 4 *qīrāṭs* ($q\bar{\imath}r\bar{a}\underline{t} = \frac{1}{24}$) of the Egyptian lands belonged to the sultan (including the fiefs of the royal mamlūks), 10 to the emirs (including the *otlāq* pasturage), 10 to the knights of *al-ḥalqa* ; in 1298 4 *qīrāṭs* were allotted to the sultan as his private domain (*al-khāṣṣ*), [4] 9 to the fiefs of the royal mamlūks and to secure their pay, 11 to the emirs and to the knights of *al-ḥalqa* ; in 1315 10 *qīrāṭs* were assigned to the royal *al-khāṣṣ*, 14 to the fiefs. Sultan al-Ashraf Sha'bān diminished the extent of *al-khāṣṣ*, granting many lands as fiefs to his brothers and relatives, [5] but it retained such towns as Alexandria, Rosetta, and Damietta. [6] The domains of *al-khāṣṣ* in Syria and in Palestine were also enlarged in 1313 by the addition of the fertile plain of Damascus and of the villages which were employed as stations of post-horses on the route from Damascus to Egypt. Even more important was the fact that the feudatories received now fiefs consisting of

---

[1] *Khiṭaṭ*, i, p. 88. *Sulūk*, ii, ii, p. 65. A. F., iv, p. 39. Ibn Khaldūn, v, p. 410. *Ṣubḥ*, iii, p. 436. Anonym, p. 45. Ibn Yaḥyā, p. 96. Ibn Iyās, i, p. 137 ; iv, p. 487. *Manhal*, v, f. 55b.

[2] Ibn Yaḥyā, pp. 79, 89–96. Anonym, p. 160. Ibn Iyās, i, p. 159. Dhahabī, ii, p. 170. Ibn Ḥajar, ii, p. 171. The local *rawk* of the governor-general of Gaza, Sanjar al-Jāwlī (*Manhal*, i, f. 16a), was possibly a part of the general.

[3] *Khiṭaṭ*, i, pp. 88–91, 95 ; ii, pp. 217–19. Anonym, p. 164. Ibn Iyās, i, p. 159. *Ṣubḥ*, iii, p. 436 ; xiii, p. 181. Ibn al-Jī'ān, pp. 99, 106, 129, 138, 139 (also merely *al-rawk* : pp. 5–7, 39, 116–17, 125, 127, 135–6, 171, 185). Ibn Ḥajar, i, p. 359. *Manhal*, v, f. 204a.

[4] These domains, inherited by the subsequent sultans, must not be confounded with the sultan's allodial estates, inherited by his heirs. After the establishment of d. *al-khāṣṣ* the domains of *al-khāṣṣ* became its principal source of revenue. The distribution of lands into *qīrāṭs* was probably based on the statistics regarding their *'ibra* and not their extent. The diminution of the fiefs of the emirs and of the knights of *al-ḥalqa* in 1298 cost to Sultan Lājīn his throne and head, though he made a concession and allotted 11 *qīrāṭs* to these fiefs instead of the originally intended 10.

[5] Cf. *Manhal*, iii, f. 151b, and the index of personal names in Ibn al-Jī'ān.

[6] Ẓāhirī, p. 108. Ibn al-Jī'ān, p. 138.

small portions dispersed in various places, where the lords, moreover, were strangers.[1] The remoteness of city-dwelling small feudatories from their fiefs obliged them, prior and subsequently to the *rawks*, to put their fiefs under the protection (*himāya*) of stronger persons, who managed the fiefs in return for a fee levied by them from the peasants and deducted from the rents transferred by them to the feudatories. In 1298 the government abolished the rule that the "emirs of 100" protected the fiefs of those knights of *al-ḥalqa* who were commanded by them,[2] and afterwards the principal protector was the sultan himself through the medium of his bureaux : *d. al-khāṣṣ, d. al-dawla, d. al-mufrad, d. al-dhakhīra*, and a special *d. al-musta'jarāt wa-l-ḥimāyāt al-sharīfa*, founded by Sultan Faraj, which had in every town and great village of Egypt its representative, *ustādār*.[3] The administrative authorities were dissatisfied with the "protection", because the local officials entrusted with it did not permit them to arrest anybody in the protected lands ; the feudatories—because the protector often took the whole revenue for himself.[4] The right of "protection" could be transferred by one person (or institution) to another, and sometimes the government even granted it as a portion of a fief, the protection fee being included in the total *'ibra* of that fief.[5]

Those fief-holders of whom the sultan was particularly suspicious were the governors-general, district governors, and tribal chieftains. Although each governor-general was

[1] Ibn Yaḥyā, p. 91, ll. 7–8.

[2] *Khiṭaṭ*, i, p. 88, ll. 5–10.

[3] Ẓāhirī, p. 97, l. 16 ; p. 107, l. 8 ; p. 108, l. 7 ; p. 109, ll. 12–13 ; p. 130, ll. 12–13. *Khiṭaṭ*, i, p. 111, ll. 26–8. *Ḥawādith*, p. 253, l. 15 ; p. 318, l. 23. Ibn Iyās, iv, p. 262.

[4] *Khiṭaṭ*, i, p. 88, ll. 5–7. *Ṣubḥ*, vii, p 206, ll. 2–4. *Ḥawādith*, p. 458 ll. 22–3. Ibn Iyās, iv, p. 485, l. 12.

[5] *Nujūm*, vi, p. 585, ll. 9–10. On emirs who "protected" entire districts, cf. *Sulūk*, I, i, p. 211 ; Ibn Ḥajar, i, p. 478, ll. 3–4. On Quatremère's attempts to explain the term *ḥimāya*, cf. *Sulūk*, I, i, pp. 211, 251 ; I, ii, p. 147 ; II, ii, p. 129.

designated as " the king of the emirs ", *malik al-umarā'*,[1] the emirs of his province were not his vassals but the sultan's, and the document (*taqlīd*) which conferred upon him the administrative authority over the province was distinct from his feudal charter, though issued simultaneously. In Egypt there were in the fourteenth century fiefs attached to the governorships, but they were scattered (partly or entirely) outside the districts ruled by the respective governors[2]; at the time of Ibn al-Jī'ān these particular fiefs were no more existing, and the governors received fiefs on the same conditions as other feudatories.[3] In Syria and in Palestine there were until the end of the Mamlūk epoch fiefs connected with the offices of governors-general and governors,[4] but it was not a common feature.[5] We learn from the feudal charters quoted by Ibn Yaḥyā that under the Ayyūbids and the first Mamlūk sultans the Lebanese tribal chieftains had no fixed military duties, except the communication of intelligence regarding the activities of the Crusaders.[6] On the occasion of the conquest of Tripoli in

---

[1] Ibn Taghrī Birdī deplores the fact that in his times this title was appropriated by district governors as well, even by those who were not appointed directly by the sultan but by some governor-general (*Ḥawādith* pp. 574–6, 672 ; cf. *Sulūk*, I, ii, pp. 96–9, n. 113).

[2] Ibn al-Jī'ān, p. 22, l. 17 ; p. 52, l. 17 ; p. 56, l. 2 ; p. 66, l. 25 ; p. 102, l. 7 ; p. 103, l. 27 ; p. 115, l. 8 ; p. 121, l. 13 ; p. 156, l. 16, etc. Only the oases of the Libyan desert were granted as fiefs to their governors : *Ta'rīf*, p. 175, ll. 18–20.

[3] The only Egyptian fief attached to an administrative post was then the fief of *zimām al-ādur al-sharīfa*, emir-eunuch entrusted with the sultan's harem : pp. 144, 168, 176, 194. As exception, the village Qaṭyā near Pelusium (where duties on the goods transported from Syria to Egypt and from Egypt to Syria were levied) was granted in A.H. 916 as fief to the emir who commanded the local garrison : Ibn Iyās, iv, pp. 192–3, 368.

[4] Ibn al-Shiḥna, p. 47, ll. 14–15 ; p. 261, ll. 3–5. Mujīr, p. 423, ll. 6–7. The military judge of Aleppo also had a particular fief : Ibn al-Shiḥna p. 232, l. 10.

[5] Under Khushqadam the governors-general of al-Karak received fiefs of " emirs of 100 " in the province of Damascus : *Ḥawādith*, p. 482, l. 12 ; p. 508, ll. 15–20.

[6] As Lebanon's destiny was not clear, B. Buḥtur used at same time from the Latin rulers, from

1289, which made the Mamlūks much more powerful in the Lebanon, Qalāūn confiscated all the fiefs of the Lebanese chieftains and transformed them into the reserve of lands for the newly established *al-ḥalqa* of Tripoli.[1] Afterwards the chieftains gradually recovered most of their fiefs, but this time they were created knights of *al-ḥalqa* or emirs of specified grades, ordered to maintain mamlūk troops corresponding to their rank, and made responsible for the watch of roads and shores in specified regions.[2] Often the village where a chieftain dwelt was not included in his fief, and he was there a tenant of another fief-holder.[3] From the data compiled by Ibn al-Jī'ān we may deduce that the bedouin fiefs in Egypt occupied in the fifteenth century a considerably greater portion of total lands than in the fourteenth, chiefly because the authorities while cruelly punishing the common bedouin rebels sought to attract the sympathy of chieftains.[4]

As the contingent of troops was not fixed, the number of fiefs was also changeable: sometimes a fief corresponding to a higher grade was created through the addition of several

Mamlūk sultans (since Aybak) and from the Ayyūbid sultan of Damascus, and they obtained a charter even from the Mongol general Hūlāgū, who invaded Syria in 1260 : Ibn Yaḥyā, pp. 55–8, 61, 64, 80.

[1] Ibn Yaḥyā, pp. 77–8, 90. Ibn Ḥajar, ii, p. 55. The only exception was the fief of a certain Ibn al-Mu'īn.

[2] Ibn Yaḥyā, pp. 31, 42–3, 78, 89, 91, 134. Ibn Ḥajar, ii, p. 55. Shidyāq, p. 231. In 1313 the contingent of mamlūks whom the chieftains had to maintain was increased (Ibn Yaḥyā, p. 89, l. 22, to p. 90, l. 3 ; p. 90, l. 23). The more influential chieftains used to receive the humbler into their service as mamlūks (p. 97, l. 3 ; p. 98, ll. 2–10).

[3] After the *rawk* a Buḥturī chieftain, Nāṣir al-Dīn, was in his own village (A'bayh) a tenant of a " Turkish " emir, Ṣārūja, whereas another chieftain, Sayf al-Dīn Mufrij, was in his own village ('Arāmūn) a tenant of Nāṣir al-Dīn (Ibn Yaḥyā, pp. 93, 102–3 ; on Ṣārūja, cf. Ibn Ḥajar, ii, p. 198, No. 1954).

[4] In A.H. 754 there were executed in Upper Egypt 700 rebels, but their chieftain, Ibn al-Aḥdab, was amnestied and returned to his post : Ibn Iyās, i, p. 200, ll. 22–4. In al-Sharqiyya the bedouin chieftains held in 1375 (either entirely or partly) 140 *nāḥiyas* (territorial divisions, mostly identical with large villages), the registered *'ibra* of which amounted to 263, 384 *d.j.*, and at the time of Ibn al-Jī'ām 189 *nāḥiyas*, the registered *'ibra* of which amounted to 393, 212 *d.j.*

small fiefs, sometimes a large fief was divided into several fiefs corresponding to a lower grade.[1] Sometimes two or several tribal chieftains held a single fief in common (*shirka, munāṣafa*), and the grade of each of them was determined by his share (*qisma*) of the fief.[2] There were no fixed rules in regard to the promotion of knights and emirs to higher grades (and fiefs connected with them).[3] Under the first Mamlūk sultans fiefs were hereditary, subject to loyal behaviour of their holders and to physical ability of the heirs to perform the military duties of knights.[4] During the lifetime of emirs their sons received, when children, allowances of money, meat, bread, and forage from the sultan, and when they became adults they were dubbed knights of *al-ḥalqa*.[5] Afterwards the emirs were for the most part selected among the royal mamlūks,[6] because of their good military training and of their personal attachment to their former master, to whom they owed their career. The comradeship [7] of the freedmen of the same master made them a real political party, seeking to turn to their exclusive advantage the great distributions of fiefs which took place when a sultan (on his accession or in the case of a civil war) wished to acquire strong and numerous supporters, an emir struggled for the regency or the crown, or many fiefs became vacant, after their holders had been killed in war or died of plague.[8] Under the Circassian sultans the

---

[1] *Hawādith*, pp. 28, 322, 393, 510, 512, 557, 601–2. Ibn Yaḥyā, p. 84, ll. 11–12. Ibn Ḥajar, i, p. 478, l. 4.

[2] Ibn Yaḥyā, pp. 154, 156, 159, 164, 166, 178, 192, 194. *Ṣubḥ*, xii, p. 423, l. 14.

[3] We know cases of suicide and murder by exasperated candidates: Ibn Iyās, i, p. 205 ; ii, pp. 225, 255, 295.

[4] *Sulūk*, i, i, pp. 233–4, 237 ; i, ii, pp. 17–18. *Ta'rīf*, p. 93, ll. 6–7.

[5] *Khiṭaṭ*, ii, p. 216, ll. 18–24. *Ḍaw' al-Ṣubḥ*, i, p. 258, ll. 18–20.

[6] *Ṣubḥ*, iv, p. 15, ll. 18–19, and the biographical dictionaries (*Manhal*, Sakhāwī, Ibn Ḥajar).

[7] " *Khushdāshiyya* " ; on the etymology of this term, cf. *Sulūk*, i, i, pp. 43–5, n. 61.

[8] Ibn Iyās, i, pp. 130, 132, 139, 190, 211, 213 216, 240, 260, 280, 352, 381 ; ii, pp. 3, 11, 12, 16, 25, 41, 72, 93, 241, 277, 305. *Sulūk*, i, ii, p. 174. *Nujūm*, vi, pp. 9, 246, *Hawādith*, pp. 178, 183, 188, 334–6, 410, 620.

Caucasian nobility had the right of priority to fiefs,[1] which was often contested by the freedmen of the reigning sultan.[2] The intervention of an influential person was also of much help in receiving a fief,[3] and often fiefs were simply sold, the seller being either the sultan in person [4] or the former holder. Many fiefs of *al-ḥalqa* were acquired by native officials (religious and civil) and merchants, who received in this way some rights of knights,[5] and by private mamlūks, who remained in the service of their lords.[6] As *awlād al-nās*, who continued to receive fiefs of *al-ḥalqa*,[7] became more and more a part of the civil population,[8] *al-ḥalqa* gradually became a corps of no military value. In the fifteenth century its knights still had at least to send to war deputies or representatives (one to every two or four holders of small fiefs) or to pay for their exemption from service,[9] but during the last Mamlūk-Ottoman war nothing of the kind was demanded from them. Fiefs of emirs and royal mamlūks also could be sold,[10] but such a fief-holder owed active military service, and in the case of his physical disability (blindness, chronic skin disease, weakness of old age, or even long

---

A. F., iv, p. 36. In the fifteenth century all the members of such a party had the same blazon (Mayer, pp. 3, 33).

[1] *Manhal*, iii, f. 186*a*, ll. 18–23. Ẓāhirī, p. 115, ll. 18–19.

[2] *Ḥawādith*, pp. 334–6. Ibn Iyās, iv, pp. 107, 342, 356, 358.

[3] Anonym, p. 46, l. 3. *Manhal*, v, f. 197*a*, ll. 17–20.

[4] Ibn Iyās, i, p. 184. *Ḥawādith*, pp. 339, 596.

[5] *Ṣubḥ*, iv, p. 16, l. 5. *Ḍaw' al-Ṣubḥ*, i, p. 245, ll. 13–14. Ibn Ḥajar, iv, p. 361, l. 9. Ibn Iyās, i, p. 198, l. 7. Sakhāwī, viii, p. 282, l. 8. Sometimes there was a special department (*dīwān al-badal*) for these transfers: *Khiṭaṭ*, ii, p. 219 (cf. Sakhāwī, x, p. 109, l. 9 : *dallāl al-iqṭā'āt* = the broker of fiefs). *Nujūm*, v, pp. 40, 423, calls it *d. al-badhl*, " the office of bribery."

[6] The right to be at the same time private mamlūks and knights of *al-ḥalqa* was acquired by them in A.H. 678 and revoked in A.H. 821 : *Sulūk*, II, i, p. 17 ; *Nujūm*, vi, pp. 386–7.

[7] Ibn Iyās, iv, p. 136, l. 5 ; p. 150, l. 13.

[8] Cf. ibid., p. 136, ll. 9–10 ; p. 150, ll. 17–18.

[9] Ibn Iyās, i, p. 331 ; ii, pp. 105, 230. *Nujūm*, vi, pp. 71, 388–9.

[10] *Ḥawādith*, pp. 339, 596, 690. *Nujūm*, vi, p. 387. In this way some *awlād al-nās* became royal mamlūks (*Ḥawādith*, p. 681).

sickness) the fief was taken back by the sultan.[1] Fiefs allotted
to tribal chieftains could be sold by their holders,[2] and granted
by the sultan (together with the offices attached to them)
to whom he wished[3]; but in general they remained vested
in families belonging to the respective tribes.

The fief was granted in response to either (*a*) a *qiṣṣa*,
written application submitted by the candidate to a vacant
fief, or (*b*) a *nuzūl*, announcement of the former feudatory
that he wishes to surrender his fief to another person, or
(*c*) an *ishhād*, notice of two feudatories who desired to exchange
their fiefs or to hold them in common, or (*d*) a *mithāl*, written
by *nāẓir al-jaysh* on the sultan's order (if the initiative
belonged to the government). In all four cases the sultan
(and in the case of small fiefs the vice-sultan) had to write
on the document his approval (*al-khaṭṭ al-sharīf*, *'alāma*,
yuktab), which contained only the word *yuktab*, "it must be
written." The approved document remained in custody
of some clerk of *d. al-jaysh*, who wrote then a new document,
al-murabba'a al-jayshiyya (sometimes denoted also as *mithāl
murabba'* or *mustanad*), which contained the sultan's order "to
grant to X the fief which had been held by Y and consisted of such-and-such villages" (or other sources of revenue).
This document was sent by *d. al-jaysh* to the sultan's chancellery (*dīwān al-inshā'*), the chief of which designated the clerk
in whose custody it was to remain and who had to write the
feudal charter, *manshūr*. The charter was practically a copy of
al-murabba'a, preceded with numerous praises to the feudatory.
The length of this preface, its opening words ("*al-ḥamd li-llāh*,"
"*ammā ba'd*," or "*kharaja l-amr*") and the size of the paper upon

---

[1] A. F., iv, p. 54. *Nujūm*, vi, p. 856. *Ḥawādith*, pp. 215, 364, 511, 577.
Manhal, ii, f. 31*a*; iv, f. 4*a*. In exceptional cases sons of sultans were
dubbed emirs in their childhood (A. F., iv, p. 92. l. 22; al-Ghawrī's son
became *amīr akhūr kabīr*, emir-inspector of royal stables).

[2] Ibn Yaḥyā, pp. 154, 184, 186–8, 192, 194.

[3] Sultan Qāïtbāy made some of his mamlūks *shaykhs* of bedouin tribes,
and gave to Yashbak al-Dawādār the post of the emir of the Hawwāra
tribe: Ibn Iyās, ii, pp. 171, 302.

which the charter was written varied according to the grade of the feudatory. Prior to the reign of al-Ashraf Sha'bān the charters of " emirs of 100 " and *al-ṭabl.* were distinguished also by *ṭughrā*, a piece of paper upon which the sultan's name and titles were written. The formula of approval (*'alāma*) which the sultan wrote on the charter consisted of some religious sentence, e.g. *ḥasbī Allāh* (Aybak), *al-musta'ān bi-llāh* (Baybars I), *Allāh amalī* (Muḥammad b. Qalāūn). In the case of the Syro-Palestinian and Lebanese knights of *al-ḥalqa, al-murabba'a al-jayshiyya* (denoted in this case also as *ruq'a*) was written in the local branch of *d. al-jaysh* in virtue of a *qiṣṣa, nuzūl, ishhād,* or *mithāl* approved by the governor-general; but then it was sent to Cairo, where it was dealt with as usual *mithāl*. The private mamlūks received their feudal charters from their lords and not from the sultan's *d. al-inshā'*. The emirs were, however, bound to inform *d. al-jaysh* whenever they received a mamlūk in their service or discharged him.[1] The investiture of an emir included the presentation to him of a horn and a flag.[2]

---

[1] For fuller particulars see Nuwayrī, viii, pp. 207–210 ; *Khiṭaṭ,* ii, pp. 216–17 ; *Ta'rīf,* pp. 88–90 ; *Ṣubḥ,* iv, 19, 51, 184, 190, 217 ; vi, pp. 201–2, 212, 223 ; xii, p. 218 ; xiii, pp. 153–199 ; Ibn Yaḥyā (the charters quoted) ; *Sulūk,* i, i, pp. 200–1 ; i, ii, p. 97 ; Ẓāhirī, p. 100, ll. 14–15 ; *Ḥawādiṯh,* p. 335, ll. 15–17. " *Yuktabāt* " in Ibn Iyās, iv, p. 136, l. 7, is not an error as the editor thinks. The sales of fiefs were usually made valid by a *nuzūl.* The Druse emirs, entitled by their religious law to distribute their estates among the heirs according to their own decision (cf. Bouron, p. 314, and Volney, ii, p. 73), used to carry this distribution into effect by a *nuzūl* when they were still living. Simultaneously they wrote a testament (*kitāb tamlīk, nuzūl*), which remained in the custody of their family and contained the same directions (Ibn Yaḥyā, pp. 56, 60, 81, 130). The verb is employed as follows : *nazala 'an . . . li. . . .*

[2] " *Ummira bi-l-būq wa-l-'alam* " : *Ṣubḥ,* iv, p. 70, ll. 2, 7, 9, 18.

III. The Decline of the Military Fiefs

After the abolition of the hereditary character of fiefs, the
feudatories struggled for the power to convey to their
descendants at least a portion of their estates as lands uncon-
ditioned by service. This struggle was facilitated by the
existence of the particular category of estates granted as
pension, *arzāq* or *rizaq* (sing. *rizq* or *rizqa*),[1] which were sub-
divided into (a) military, *al-rizaq al-jayshiyya*[2] or *akhbāz*,[3]
and (b) religious, *al-rizaq al-aḥbāsiyya*[4] or *aḥbās*.[5] In both
cases they were lands granted away by the state not on the
condition of military (or other) service but " as charity ",
'alā sabīl al-birr wa-l-ṣadaqa.[6] *Al-rizaq al-jayshiyya* were
fiefs granted away by *d. al-jaysh* to (a) emirs who could no
more perform military duties because of their old age or
illness[7]; (b) emirs who for political reasons were dismissed
and then, for the most part, relegated to Jerusalem[8]; (c) wives,

[1] *Ḥawādith*, p. 57, l. 17; p. 410, ll. 13–17; p. 577, ll. 16–17 (*istarzaqa* =
derived an income from a *rizq*). Ibn Iyās, iv, p. 15, ll. 11, 18; p. 136,
ll. 4–19; p. 150, ll. 13–18.

[2] Ibn Iyās, v, p. 420, ll. 7–9; p. 475, ll. 18–19; p. 480, l. 20.

[3] *Sulūk*, I, ii, pp. 159–161. The same word denoted sometimes all the
fiefs.

[4] Nuwayrī, viii, p. 209, l. 1. Ibn Khaldūn, v, p. 410, l. 11. *Khiṭaṭ*, i,
p. 110, l. 17. Ibn Iyās, iv, p. 136; v, pp. 219, 460–1, 466, 475, 480.

[5] On their identity with *al-rizaq al-aḥbāsiyya*, cf. Ẓāhirī, p. 109, ll. 13–14;
Ibn Iyās, v, p. 461, ll. 1–3.

[6] *Ṣubḥ*, iv, p. 38, ll. 7–16. *Ḍaw' al-Ṣubḥ*, i, p. 250, ll. 22–3. *Nujūm*, vi,
p. 69, ll. 7–8. Almost in the same words Jabartī, iv, p. 93, ll. 19, 31; p. 141,
l. 32. Hence the adjective *al-mabrūra*, employed in official documents in
regard to these lands: *Ṣubḥ*, vi, p. 185, ll. 16–20.

[7] Under the sultans Jaqmaq and Khushqadam such an estate brought
about 200,000 dirhems yearly: *Ḥawādith*, p. 511, ll. 8–9; p. 577, l. 17.
A retired emir (or knight), who was entitled to dwell wherever he liked,
was denoted as *tarkhān* (*Ṣubḥ*, xiii, p. 48), whereas the term *baṭṭāl* designated
especially him who was dismissed and banished.

[8] *Ṣubḥ*, vii, p. 200, ll. 9–17. These estates were situated in those parts
of Palestine which were included in the province of Damascus (*Ṣubḥ*, xii,
p. 314, l. 7). On Jerusalem as the principal place of banishment for emirs,
cf. *Manhal*, i, ff. 27a, 158a, 162a, 196b, 197a, 200a;
37a, 44a, 89b, etc.

widows, and orphans of emirs and knights [1] ; (*d*) *awlād al-nās*, including the descendants of sultans [2] ; (*e*) mosques, madrasas, monasteries of dervishes, learned and holy persons.[3] Sometimes such a fief, although explicitly not conditional upon service, was considered as an emir's fief or a fief of *al-ḥalqa*, and its holder obtained a *manshūr* [4] ; but for the most part the holder was not entitled to a military grade, and he received from *d. al-jaysh* a particular charter, denoted as *al-murabba‘a al-jayshiyya*,[5] which must not be confused with the abovementioned document of the same name. In the work of Ibn al-Jī‘ān we find a multitude of cases that in a *nāḥiya* which contained hundreds or thousands of *faddāns* there was a *rizq* of several tens of *faddāns*, the holder of which is never mentioned, being probably identical with the explicitly indicated lord of the village. We may assume that the lord wished to strengthen his right of possession by the unconditional tenure of some important place in the village (well, irrigating channel, houses).

The word *aḥbās* being employed as synonymous for *waqfs* by the Mālikī school of the Islamic law, the only school which permits the conversion of the revenues of leased lands into a *waqf* for the period of lease, we are inclined to believe that the appearance of *aḥbās* as a particular category of lands took place under the Fāṭimids, when the Mālikī school was the only Sunnī school recognized by the courts of justice,[6] and the fiefs were still conditional not on military service but on payment of rents.[7] Indeed, though there are sources

---

[1] Ibn Iyās, iv, p. 15, ll. 12–13 ; p. 16, ll. 4–5 ; p. 136, l. 5 ; p. 150, ll. 15–16 ; v, p. 219, ll. 7–8.

[2] *Manhal*, i, f. 55*b*, ll. 8–9.

[3] *Ṣubḥ*, iv, p. 51, l. 19 ; vi. p. 185, l. 19.

[4] Sakhāwī, iii, p. 2, l. 11. Ibn Ḥajar. ii, p. 214, l. 17. Ibn Iyās, iv, p. 136, ll. 4–19 ; p. 150, ll. 13–18. The term *akhbāz* is employed for the most part in regard to these estates.

[5] Ibn Iyās, v, p. 189, ll. 16–20 ; p. 218, l. 23, to p. 219, l. 1 ; p. 219, l. 6 ; p. 287, l. 17. Ẓāhirī, p. 100, ll. 19–20. Women and institutions could not receive *manshūrs* at all.

[6] *Ṣubḥ*, iii, p. 524, l. 13.

[7] *Khiṭaṭ*, i, p. 85, ll. 35–6, 39.

which ascribe the foundation of *dīwān al-aḥbās* to such an early personage as al-Layth b. Sa'd, the *qāḍī* of Egypt in the second century A.H.,[1] or to such a late as Saladin,[2] the notice which attributes it to the Fāṭimids[3] is corroborated by other texts which attest the existence of particular *aḥbās*-lands under the Fāṭimids.[4] In the Mamlūk epoch they were royal lands dedicated to religious institutions and persons of merit, and considered as of more holy character than *al-rizaq al-jayshiyya*, though not attaining the rank of genuine *waqfs*. They were supervised by a special royal office, *dīwān al-aḥbās*, the director (*nāẓir*) of which was considered as a religious official, and was sometimes responsible to the Grand Dawādār (= the emir who supervised the royal chancellery)—who, since A.H. 768, occasionally held himself this post—and sometimes before the vice-sultan or the sultan in person.[5] Owing to the constant increase of these estates they amounted already in A.H. 740 to 130,000 *faddāns*,[6] and at the time of the Ottoman conquest there were in Upper Egypt alone 1,800 such *rizaq*.[7] The *aḥbās* held by the Christian churches and monasteries in Egypt were seized in A.H. 759 and distributed among the emirs as addition to their fiefs.[8] The charter granted to a holder of such an estate was designated as *tawqī' aḥbāsī* and emanated from *dīwān al-aḥbās*.[9] In Syria, Palestine, and the Lebanon the extent of *aḥbās* was much smaller than in Egypt.[10]

[1] Ibn Iyās, v, p. 461, ll. 1–3.

[2] Jabartī, iv, p. 93, l. 26.

[3] *Khiṭaṭ*, ii, p. 295, l. 5.

[4] Ibid., i, p. 110, ll. 4–17. J. Mann, *The Jews in Egypt and in Palestine under the Fāṭimid Caliphs*, Oxford, 1922, ii, p. 354 (Jewish *aḥbās* in Palestine). Ibn Khallikān, *Wafayāt al-A'yān*, ii, p. 166.

[5] *Ṣubḥ*, iv, p. 38, ll. 7–16. *Ḍaw' al-Ṣubḥ*, i, p. 250, ll. 21–4. Ẓāhirī, p. 109, ll. 13–15. *Khiṭaṭ*, ii, p. 295. *Sulūk*, I, i, p. 119, n. 2. Ibn Iyās, i, p. 220, ll. 1–2.

[6] *Khiṭaṭ*, ii, p. 295, l. 31.

[7] Ibn Iyās, v, p. 461, ll. 6, 22–3.

[8] Ibid., i, p. 206, ll. 6–11 (their total size was then 20,000 *faddāns*).

[9] Ẓāhirī, p. 109, l. 15.

[10] Nuwayrī, viii, p. 209, ll. 1–2. Cf. *Sulūk*, I, ii, p. 59, n. 71.

Among the estates granted as pension we may place the caliph's fief. Though the founder of the Mamlūk state, Aybak, proclaimed when fighting against the dynastic pretensions of the Syrian Ayyūbids that " the country belongs to the caliph, and the king is only his representative " [1]— when the seat of the caliphate was transferred in 659/1261 to Egypt, the caliphs did not receive there any landed estate. It was Barqūq [2] who revived the practice, which existed in Iraq since A.H. 334 [3] and in Egypt under the last Fāṭimids,[4] that the powerless caliph obtains from the real ruler an *iqtāʻ*.[5] As a fief-holder the caliph was considered a member of the military class, and he possessed in consequence a coat of arms (*rank*).[6] The caliph's fief was enlarged by Sultan Yūsuf in A.H. 841, by Aynāl in A.H. 857 (in reward for the caliph's assistance to his accession) and by Aynāl's son, Aḥmad, but it was reduced again by Qāïtbāy in A.H. 872.[7] When first the caliph al-Mutawakkil was exiled to Constantinople after the conquest of Egypt by the Ottomans, he held his Egyptian fief, but afterwards Sultan Selīm I ordered him to divide it with two other exiled ʻAbbāsids.[8] We do not know whether there was any connection between this fief and the landed estates held by the descendants of the Egyptian ʻAbbāsids in the eighteenth century.[9]

---

[1] And this function may be, consequently, performed by any person appointed by the caliph : A. F., iii, p. 192, l. 12 ; *Manhal*, i, f. 3*a*, l. 17.

[2] *Khiṭaṭ*, ii, p. 243, ll. 20–1. Ibn al-Jīʻān does not mention any estate as held by the caliph in 1375.

[3] A. F., ii, p. 100, l. 7. Abū Shāma, *Kitāb al-Rawḍatayn*, Cairo, A.H. 1287–1292, i, p. 31, l. 30.

[4] Abū Shāma, i, p. 196, l. 19.

[5] " *Iqtāʻ al-khilāfa* " : Ibn Iyās, ▼, p. 347, l. 23.

[6] Ibid., p. 155, l. 4.

[7] *Nujūm*, vii, p. 6, l. 1 ; p. 461, l. 2. *Ḥawādith*, p. 236, l. 6 ; p. 382, l. 1 ; p. 633, ll. 3–8. Ibn Iyās, ii, p. 51, l. 8 ; p. 96, ll. 15–18 ; iv, p. 292, ll. 1–6. Sakhāwī, iii, p. 166, l. 21. At the time of Ibn al-Jīʻān it consisted of two entire villages and of portions of two others (p. 25, l. 15 ; p. 80, l. 18 ; p. 144, l. 10 ; p. 158, l. 7).

[8] Ibn Iyās, v, pp. 312–13, 347–8.

[9] Jabartī, iii, p. 355, l. 32.

Since *al-rizaq al-jayshiyya* could be taken back by the state,[1] the best way open to the feudatories who wished to convert their military fiefs into lifelong and hereditary possessions was to make them allodial lands, *amlāk* (sing. *mulk*). At the commencement of the Mamlūk epoch allodial estates were numerous in Syria,[2] but almost absent in Egypt.[3] Their subsequent increase, mostly through the addition of former military fiefs,[4] was a direct violation of the Islamic law which forbids the transformation of " tribute-paying " lands into " tithe-paying " (allodial).[5] The lawyers of the Mamlūk epoch abrogated this rule : the right given by the Islamic law to the caliph to grant away unowned and conquered lands to Moslems as allodial properties was extended to all lands reverting to the state for any reason whatever, the caliph being represented by the administration of the public treasury (*bayt al-māl*), appointed in reality by the sultan. In particular they utilized the theory that every property the owner of which died without leaving heirs, becomes the property (*mulk*) of the whole Moslem community,[6] and the question whether the caliph is entitled to sell such lands was always answered in the affirmative. Moreover, the fief-holder who surrendered his fief to the public treasury of his own free will was entitled to purchase it then as allodial estate or to arrange its purchase by a friend.[7] Lands which became allodial because of their

---

[1] Ibn Iyās, iv, pp. 136, 150, 321–2 ; v, p. 90. *Al-rizaq al-ahbāsiyya* were held for the most part by religious officials and institutions (cf. *Hawādith*, p. 140, l. 8 ; *Daw'*, i, p. 250, ll. 22–3).

[2] Ibn al-Shihna, p. 128, ll. 8–10 ; p. 168, l. 8 ; p. 174, ll. 7–8 (quotations from Ibn Shaddād, a contemporary of Baybars I : p. 170, ll. 2, 13).

[3] *Subh*, iii, p. 455, ll. 10–12. The old allodial lands were there converted under the Fāṭimids into " tribute-paying " lands : *Khitat*, i, p. 84, ll. 2–8.

[4] *Nujūm*, vi, p. 387, l. 17.

[5] Under the Mamlūks no fixed tax was imposed by the government on the allodial lands (or any other lands which were not held by the crown). Sometimes they paid extraordinary taxes.

[6] Cf. *Subh*, xiii, p. 115, ll. 3–8.

[7] Ibn Yaḥyā, p. 102, l. 13, to p. 103, l. 1. It is possible that the conversion of " tribute-paying " lands into allodial through their sale by the public

sale by the public treasury were very numerous,[1] and were often purchased by the sultan, either for himself[2] or as gifts to influential emirs.[3]

Many fiefs and royal estates were transformed into *waqfs*.[4] In the fifteenth century the overlords often founded endowments for the sake of their mamlūks,[5] in order to make the latter more devoted to them and to their descendants. Sometimes the descendants of founders were the beneficiaries of their *waqfs*,[6] but more often the *waqfs* were dedicated to some social or religious objective—e.g. the defence of coasts against European corsairs,[7] the payment of ransom for the Moslems captured by them,[8] water supply,[9] hospitals,[10]

treasury was among the usages brought by the Mamlūks from Turkestan (then partly ruled by the Golden Horde), where this custom still existed in the nineteenth century. Cf. M. N. Rostislavov, *Očerk vidov zemelnoĭ sobstvennosti i pozemelnyĭ vopros v Turkestanskom kraĭe*, St. Petersburg, 1879, pp. 7–8.

[1] Ibn al-Jī'ān, p. 5, l. 22 ; p. 9, l. 9 ; p. 11, l. 23 ; p. 14, l. 31 ; p. 106, l. 24 ; p. 109, l. 22 ; p. 114, l. 24 ; p. 130, l. 21 ; p. 130, l. 10 ; p. 194, l. 5. Ibn Ḥabīb, *Durrat al-Aslāk* (*Orientalia*, ii, 1846), p. 381, ll. 23–4.

[2] *Sulūk*, ɪ, ii, p. 76.

[3] Palmyra was bought by Qalāūn for the chief emir of Āl Faḍl (*Manhal*, iv, f. 202a, ll. 22–3).

[4] This term and the verb *waqafa* are sometimes employed in Mamlūk sources with regard to estates granted as pension (*Ḥawādith*, p. 418, l. 8 ; Ibn al-Jī'ān, p. 25, l. 15 ; p. 80, l. 18 ; p. 144, l. 10 ; p. 158, l. 7 ; Ibn Iyās, iv, p. 15, ll. 10–12, 16 ; p. 150, l. 16 ; v, p. 395, ll. 13–14 ; *Ṣubḥ*, iv, p. 55, l. 13). The principal distinction between them and the genuine *waqfs* was that a genuine *waqf* was established by the land-holder (who might originally convert the land into allodial), and the pension estate by the crown. On the increase of genuine *waqfs*, cf. Ibn al-Jī'ān, p. 147, ll. 17, 20 ; p. 149, ll. 3, 26 ; p. 150, ll. 3, 15, etc. *Khiṭaṭ*, i, p. 110, ll. 28–30.

[5] Ibn al-Jī'ān, p. 115, l. 27 ; p. 128, l. 6 ; p. 135, l. 19 ; p. 162, l. 1 ; p. 179, l. 18.

[6] *CIA.*, i, pp. 353–360, No. 247. Ibn Iyās, i, p. 225, ll. 18–19.

[7] *Manhal*, ii, f. 34a, ll. 8–9. Ibn Duqmāq, v, p. 114, l. 5. Ibn Iyās, ii, p. 189, l. 15. Cf. Ibn Yaḥyā, p. 42, ll. 10–15.

[8] *Ṣubḥ*, xii, p. 47, ll. 4–6 ; p. 52, l. 15 ; p. 391, ll. 14–15.

[9] Mayer, p. 188. Ibn Ḥajar, i, p. 285, l. 14. Bischoff, *Ta'rīkh Ḥalab*, Beirut, 1880, p. 132.

[10] Ibn Iyās, i, p. 116, l. 11. Ibn al-Shiḥna, p. 1 7, l. 5. l. 9 ; iii f. 107b.

institutions of the Hijaz,[1] and particularly mosques, madrasas, mausoleums and monasteries of dervishes.[2] The founder who wished to ensure the future of his descendants preferred to appoint them hereditary managers of the *waqf*: such managers could usually employ the revenues of *waqfs* as they liked, often transgressing the rules fixed by their founders.[3] The terminology employed in the sources of information regarding their right of management is similar to that used in describing the feudal land tenure [4]; they also employed the *nuzūl* in order to transfer the management to their sons or friends [5]; and in general we may define them as religious feudatories, whose social position (unless they held military fiefs at the same time) was humbler than that of the military, but of more hereditary character. The management of certain *waqfs* was attached to specified military posts, especially to those of the chief military judge, the Grand Dawādār, *zimām al-ādur, ra's nawbat al-nuwab* (= the commander of the royal mamlūks who guarded the palace) and the governor of Baalbek.[6] Practically all the modern aristocratic families which were already influential under the Mamlūks (except the tribal chieftains) owe their privileged position (and its survival) to their posts as hereditary managers or beneficiaries of important *waqfs*. Some of them are of " Turkish " descent, as al-Barqūqī in Egypt [7] and al-Nashāshībī in Jerusalem [8];

---

[1] *Sulūk*, pp. 69–70. *CIA.*, i, p. 346, n. 1. Ibn Duqmāq, v, pp. 33, 48, 131. Ibn Iyās, ii, p. 194, ll. 16–26.

[2] Cf. the index of such Egyptian institutions in Ibn al-Jī'ān.

[3] *Ḥawādith*, p. 17, ll. 1–3. *Manhal*, iv, f. 158a, ll. 1–2. On the Ottoman epoch, cf. Volney, ii, p. 370; Jabartī, ii, p. 127, ll. 13–15; iv, p. 189, l. 9, to p. 190, l. 1 ; Ibn al-Shiḥna, p. 117, ll. 2–12.

[4] Ibn al-Shiḥna, p. 116, l. 18 (" *wa-hiya al-ān bi-sm* " ; cf. Ibn al-Jī'ān, many times).

[5] Ibn al-Shiḥna, p. 116, ll. 5–6, 17 ; p. 117, ll. 16–20.

[6] *Ḥawādith*, p. 17, ll. 1–3 ; p. 54, ll. 2–10 ; p. 80, l. 17. Ibn Iyās, i, p. 203, l. 19 ; iv, p. 35, ll. 13–14 ; p. 317, ll. 18–19. *Ṣubḥ*, xii, p. 117, ll. 9–10 ; p. 319, ll. 3–4.

[7] The descendants of Sulṭan Barqūq, entrusted with the administration of his *waqfs*. Cf. Jabartī, iv, p. 105, ll. 22–3.

[8] The descendants of the emir Nāṣir al-Dīn Muḥammad b. Aḥmad b. Rajab, born in Cairo in A.H. 821 (probably belonged to *awlād al-nās*),

those houses which claim the descent from Muḥammad and his friends, as al-Ḥusaynī in Jerusalem [1] and al-Tamīmī in Hebron, [2] were under the Mamlūks of lower rank.

Towards the end of the Mamlūk epoch the total size of the military fiefs was already much smaller than at its commencement, [3] and the fief of a military lord was as a rule but a part (often not the greater part) of his possessions, the remainder [4] consisting of *rizaq*, allodial estates, *waqfs* founded by him and still regarded as his domains, [5] and sometimes *waqfs* managed by him. It was, however, the Ottoman conquest which brought about the complete abolition

who served between A.H. 875–893 as *nāẓir al-ḥaramayn* (superintendent of the mosques of Jerusalem and Hebron and manager of their *waqfs*) : Sakhāwī, vi, pp. 308–9, No. 1025 ; Mujīr, pp. 621–672. His coat of arms has been described by Mayer. On the post of *nāẓir al-ḥaramayn*, reserved for emirs, cf. *Ta'rīf*, pp. 108–9 ; Ṣubḥ, xii, p. 105, ll. 2–3 ; Mujīr, pp. 604–19.

[1] At the end of the thirteenth century this branch (" al-Ḥusaynī al-Wafā'ī ") of the descendants of Muḥammad's grandson, al-Ḥusayn b. 'Alī, leased the village of Sharafāt from a fief-holder, and it remained their residence and possession throughout the Mamlūk epoch. They were hereditary holders of the post of *naqīb al-ashrāf* in Jerusalem, which implied the representation of Muḥammad's descendants before the authorities and the management of endowments dedicated to them (hence they were called also B. al-Naqīb). They became particularly prominent under the Ottoman rule, when the military nobility of foreign origin lost its privileged position. Cf. Mujīr, p. 490 ; Sakhāwī, i, p. 259 ; iv, p. 309 ; Jabartī, i, pp. 66, 412, 371–4 ; ii, pp. 70–1 ; Finn, i, p. 180.

[2] The descendants of Tamīm al-Dārī, a Companion of Muḥammad. Under the Mamlūks and subsequently to them they were officials of the mosque of Hebron and recipients of the revenues of the endowment set apart, according to the tradition, by Muḥammad for their ancestor. Many of them became distinguished legists and men of letters. Cf. Ṣubḥ, xiii, p. 122, ll. 8–10. Mujīr, pp. 429, 632. Sakhāwī, i, p. 204 ; ii, p. 13 ; iv, p. 95 ; v, p. 192. al-'Umarī, *Masālik al-Abṣār*, i, Cairo, 1924, pp. 172 ff.

[3] *Nujūm*, vi, p. 387, l. 17. Cf. the detailed figures in Ibn al-Jī'ān.

[4] Ibn Iyās, i, p. 156, ll. 18–23 ; p. 172, ll. 7–14 ; p. 198, ll. 5–12 ; iv, p. 242, ll. 3–4, 14–17. *Ḥawādith*, p. 562, l. 18 ; pp. 568–9. *Manhal*, ii, ff. 86a, 160–1. Many cases in Ibn al-Jī'ān.

[5] He could even sell them as allodial estates, *Ḥawādith*, p. 167, l. 9, to p. 168, l. 3 ; p. 202, l. 13. Ibn Iyās, ii, p. 45, l. 26 ; iv, p. 109, l. 20, to p. 110, l. 3 ; p. 242, ll. 3–4. Cf. on the Ottoman epoch, Jabartī, i, p. 28, l. 30 ; p. 101, ll. 6–7. The legal pretext was that the founder was in debt at the time of the foundation, his property was then a security for the payment of his debt, and therefore the *waqf* was illegal from the beginning.

of the military fiefs in Egypt. For several months the mamlūks and their emirs (but not *awlād al-nās*) were outlawed and disguised themselves in peasant dresses.[1] The military fiefs were seized and annexed to the royal domains,[2] but *al-rizaq al-jayshiyya* (except those granted by *manshūrs*) and *al-rizaq al-aḥbāsiyya* remained intact,[3] as well as the *waqfs*. In the same year (933/1517) the mamlūks were pardoned and gradually became a part of the Ottoman garrison in Egypt (at first the amnesty entitled them only to live as civilians, afterwards they received the right to mount horses and to purchase arms, and a *nafaqa* was paid to them a little later). This action roused the indignation of the genuine Ottoman troops, who wished to obtain for themselves former privileges of the royal mamlūks, viz. their monthly pay, rations of meat and forage, and military fiefs.[4] The authorities utilized the opposing pretensions of the two parts of the garrison and did not restore the military fiefs at all. The mamlūks received an addition to their pay as compensation for their lost fiefs and for the discontinued rations of meat and forage.[5] The Ottoman Turks, who received at first only a small daily pecuniary allowance for their expenses, obtained a monthly salary, greater than the augmented pay of the mamlūks.[6] *Al-ḥalqa* was not restored, but some *awlād al-nās* were admitted into an Ottoman regiment, *al-kamūliyya*.[7] *Dīwān al-jaysh* continued for some time to sell lands to the

---

[1] Ibn Iyās, v, pp. 147–8.

[2] Ibid., p. 158, ll. 14–22 ; p. 167, l. 19 ; p. 176, ll. 9–11 ; p. 185, ll. 12–16 ; p. 186, ll. 6–9, 13–15. Hammer, i, pp. 789–790.

[3] Ibn Iyās, v, p. 189, ll. 16–20 ; p. 460, l. 22, to p. 461, l. 3. Later the Egyptian fiscal administration made several attempts to seize a portion of these estates or their revenues : pp. 218–19, 249–250, 264, 287, 332, 460–1, 466, 475, 480.

[4] Ibid., p. 209, ll. 4–14.

[5] Ibid., p. 242, ll. 16–19 ; p. 404, l. 22, to p. 405, l. 2.

[6] Ibid., p. 404, ll. 13–22.

[7] Ibid., p. 369, ll. 18–22. It   regiment, name of which was pronounced p. 193).

persons who wished to acquire them, no longer as fiefs but as *al-rizaq al-jayshiyya*; as, however, the buyers sought to transform them into allodial domains by all means in their power (including the falsification of documents), this particular category of lands gradually disappeared.[1] During the first years after the conquest, the bedouin chieftains retained their estates, and the most influential among them were appointed and supervised directly by the central government, and not through the medium of the Egyptian governor-general.[2] But since their participation in the unsuccessful revolt of the governor-general, Aḥmad-pasha, in 1524, we find them no longer as fief-holders but merely as farmers of royal estates.[3]

The Syro-Palestinian mamlūk troops retreated in 1516 to Egypt, fleeing from the Ottomans, and shared the fate of the Egyptian mamlūks. The tribal chieftains who declared their submission to the conquerors were either confirmed in the possession of their former fiefs or remunerated with additional ones. Among the former we may mention a Buḥturī chieftain, Sharaf al-Dīn Yaḥyā[4]; among the latter—the chief of B. Ma'n (Fakhr al-Dīn I) and the ancestor of the Kurdish family of Jānbulāṭ (*alias* Jānbūlād, Janbulāṭ). Both of them were made *sanjāq-bays*, i.e. governors of their respective districts (Sidon and Beirut in the Lebanon, Killis in North Syria) and holders of the fiefs attached to these posts.[5] The

---

[1] Ibn Iyās, v, p. 420, l. 5, to p. 421, l. 14 ; p. 469, ll. 1–5 ; p. 475, ll. 18–19 (the authorities gave back the estates confiscated from the falsificators !). As the genuine fiefs existed no more, Ibn Iyās often uses the term *iqṭā'āt* in regard to *al-rizaq al-jayshiyya* (e.g. p. 258, ll. 6–7 ; p. 287, l. 8) ; the same meaning it has probably in Isḥāqī, p. 136, l. 5.

[2] Ibn Iyās, v, p. 164, ll. 3–4 ; p. 269, ll. 23–4 ; p. 284, ll. 15–18 ; p. 387, ll. 13–17 ; p. 429, ll. 1–5 ; p. 431, ll. 10–20. The chiefs of B. 'Umar, B. al-Aḥdab, B. Baqar, B. Baghdād, and B. Mur'ā, were dignified in this manner.

[3] In the second half of the sixteenth century the governors of al-Manūfiyya were selected among B. Baghdād : Isḥāqī, p. 137, ll. 27–36.

[4] Shidyāq, p. 246, ll. 1–2, 10.

[5] Hammer, i, p. 764 ; ii, p. 705. " Moinoghli " is identical with Fakhr al-Dīn I, according to a local tradition (Shidyāq, p. 251, ll. 11–22) ; otherwise we should have thought of some Ibn al-Mu'īn.

governor-generalship of South Syria, Palestine, and the Lebanon was conferred in 1517 upon a mamlūk emir, Jān Birdī al-Ghazālī, whose troops consisted of those mamlūks who came from Egypt to serve him,[1] certain native auxiliaries, and a small Ottoman garrison.[2] We may assume that they were paid in cash (as Egyptian forces), excepting the tribal chieftains. After the suppression of al-Ghazālī's revolt in 1520–1 the local mamlūk corps was disbanded, and the Ottoman system of military fiefs was introduced.

According to 'Ayn-i 'Alī, the Ottoman feudal army of Syria and Palestine amounted to 8,258 horsemen: 3,194 in the province of Damascus, 1,821 in the province of Tripoli, 3,243 in the province of Aleppo. Among them there were 2,561 feudatories (1,006 in the province of Damascus, 642 in the province of Tripoli, 913 in the province of Aleppo) and 5,697 knights (jabalū) in their service. The latter were freedmen of their lords, as the former private mamlūks, but had not the same opportunity of becoming feudatories, owing to the hereditary character of the Ottoman fiefs. Nineteen fiefs were attached to the posts of governors-general and district governors; 9 to those of other high dignitaries of the provinces; 295 were held by great feudatories (zu'amā'); 2,238 by smaller (arbāb-i tīmār). The value of the fiefs was their average yearly revenue (ḥāṣil), when expressed in an Ottoman silver monetary unit, asper.[3] The revenue of a small fief (tīmār) was 2,000 aspers or more; of a large fief (zi'āmat) 20,000 or more; of a khāṣṣ (i.e. fief attached to the post of a governor-general, governor, or provincial treasurer), in the case of Syro-Palestinian provinces,

---

[1] Ibn Iyās, v, p. 377, ll. 18–19. A Palestinian family, Abū Ghawsh (pronounced Abū Ghōsh), claims descent from these mamlūks: Finn, i, pp. 229–235.

[2] Ibn Iyās, v, p. 377, ll. 17–21; p. 418, l. 7; p. 419, ll. 8–9. Hammer, ii, p. 19.

[3] On the value of asper (aqcha, al-'uthmānī), cf. Belin in JA., 6e sér., iii, pp. 422–5. It gradually became a fictitious unit, employed by the treasury and differing in various provinces, Jabartī, iii, p. 213, ll. 3–7.

it might be 113,000 to 1,000,995 aspers. Several districts were
not divided into fiefs but considered as crown domains : (*a*)
Palmyra, (*b*) Sidon and Beirut, (*c*) al-Karak and al-Shawbak
in the province of Damascus, (*d*) " the Turcomans of Aleppo
and 'Azāz ", (*e*) Manbij . and al-Maḍīq in the province of
Aleppo. From other sources we learn that there were also
considerable crown domains in other districts, e.g. the
region of Tiberias [1] and some forests in the province of
Damascus.[2] In the terms of modern political geography
there were *approximately* [3] 517 fiefs in Palestine (the districts
of Jerusalem, Gaza, Ṣafad, Nablus, and al-Lujūn), 66 in
Trans-Jordan (in the district of 'Ajlūn), 100 in the Lebanon
(in the district of Tripoli), and 202 in Cilicia (the district of
Adana), whereas about 1,676 were situated within the
boundaries of the modern Syrian Republic and Hatay (the
territory of the latter was then divided among neighbouring
districts).

'Ayn-i 'Alī wrote his book in 1609, but the figures compiled
by him are about 20 to 30 years older.[4] According to the
Ottoman feudal system the number of fiefs in each district
was relatively stable, because the nucleus of each fief (*qilīj*,
the portion from which the minimum of *ḥāṣil* assigned to
the respective grade of fiefs was derived) was to remain an
indivisible unit. 'Ayn-i 'Alī's figures relate to these units,
and therefore they probably represent the state of things

---

[1] Between 1560–1603 this region was farmed by Jewish bankers of
Constantinople : at first by Joseph ha-Nasi' (*alias* João Miquez) and his
mother-in-law, then by Solomon Ibn Ya'ish (*alias* Alvaro Mendez) and his
son. Cf. Joseph ha-Kohen, '*Emeq ha-Baka*', ed. Letteris, pp. 145–7 ;
Fr. Pantaleao de Aveiro, *Itinerario da Terra Sancta*, Lisbon, 1583,
1927 ; *Transactions of the Jewish Historical Society of England*, xi, 1928,
pp. 26 ff., 84.

[2] *JA.*, 9e sér., iv, 1894, p. 277.

[3] The modern Syro-Turkish frontier is not identical with the northern
boundary of the province of Aleppo in the sixteenth century, e.g. the town
of Killis is now within the limits of Turkey. Nor are the modern frontiers
of Syria, Palestine, and the Lebanon quite the same as the district
boundaries of 'Ayn-i 'Alī's time.

[4] Tischendorf, pp. 58, 100, 118.

which existed in the province of Aleppo after the conquest
and in the provinces of Damascus and Tripoli after the
suppression of al-Ghazālī's revolt. On the other hand, when
Ayn-i ‘Alī compiled them they were already out of date.
The emir ‘Alī of the Jānbulāṭ family tried in 1605–7 to become
an independent ruler of Syria and Palestine, captured all
three centres of provinces, and drew away the feudal troops
of the Ottomans.[1] After the suppression of this revolt we
hear no more of military fiefs ; not only Volney (1783–5)
but already such an early traveller as d'Arvieux (1664)
ignored the former existence of Ottoman military fiefs in
Syria and in Palestine.[2] We know that the Ottoman sultans
considered every country which they lost, even for two or
three years only, as an enemy's territory (*dār al-ḥarb*), the
lands of which must become on its reconquest their spoil of
war.[3] This theory was probably utilized in 1607 as the pretext
for not restoring the Syro-Palestinian military fiefs. The real
reason seems to lie in the fact that the steadily growing use of muskets considerably diminished the military
value of the cavalry, especially in the hill districts, and that
the mercenary and peasant troops of ‘Alī Jānbulāṭ overthrew
the feudal regiments thanks to the extensive use of the
infantry.[4] Owing to the relative remoteness from the Empire's
frontiers, the Syro-Palestinian military feudatories were
primarily entrusted with the suppression of local revolts ; it
now became clear that this task was beyond their powers.

---

[1] Hammer, ii, pp. 705–710. Shidyāq, pp. 132–6.

[2] Volney, ii, p. 373. Roque, p. 75.

[3] Jabartī, iv, p. 94, ll. 11–13. We find this view already under the
Mamlūks, *Sulūk*, i, ii, p. 59, n. 71.

[4] In 1664 we already hear of muskets owned by common peasants,
though the bedouins were not yet accustomed to fire-arms. Roque, p. 78.
The cavalry of ‘Alī Jānbulāṭ did not outnumber that of the enemy,
Hammer, loc. cit.

IV. The Farming of the Crown Domains

Under the Mamlūks a village which belonged to the sultan
was usually held by a farmer, who collected taxes from the
peasants and either paid annually a fixed rent after
the harvest or concluded every year a new agreement
in regard to the amount which he had to pay. The first form,
faṣl, was at first practised in the Syro-Palestinian coast
lands, and in the fifteenth century it became customary in
Egypt.[1] The second, *ḍamān*, existed in those villages of the
Damascus plain which cultivated principally fruit-trees,[2]
and probably also in other parts of the state. The farmer[3]
was either the district governor or a bedouin *shaykh*, a
religious official or another man of wealth and influence. The
manager of a royal department (*d. al-mufrad,* *d. al-dawla,*
d. al-khāṣṣ, or *d. al-dhakhīra*) acted as the chief farmer of the
villages allotted to that department and exploited them
through the medium of local farmers. Whereas during most
of the Mamlūk epoch the domains of each department were
scattered in various parts of Egypt (in Syria, Palestine, and
the Lebanon we hear only of *al-khāṣṣ*), towards its end a
chief farmer usually administered (*taḥaddatha 'alā* or *takallama
'alā*) an entire rural region, *taqsīṭ*.[4] Some of the regional
'farmers were high emirs: e.g. the royal domains in
Upper Egypt were farmed for the most part by the Grand

---

[1] Nuwayrī, viii, p. 260, l. 10, to p. 261, l. 2. Ẓāhirī, p. 130, ll. 14–21.
Faṣl is, according to Nuwayrī, a Frankish word (" vassal " ?).

[2] Anonym, p. 82, ll. 21–3. It was the system employed in the industrial
and mercantile monopolies of the sultan (*al-jihāt al-maḍmūna*, Ẓāhirī,
p. 97, ll. 17–18).

[3] He was denoted as *mutadarrik* (Ẓāhirī, p. 107, l. 9 ; p. 130, ll. 13–20.
Ḥawādith, p. 724, l. 5), *mudarrik* (*Ḥawādith*, p. 655, ll. 1–8. Ibn Iyās, iv,
p. 318, l. 1 ; p. 327, l. 7), or *'āmil* (*Nujūm*, vi, p. 399, ll. 14–20. Ibn Iyās, iv,
p. 105, l. 3 ; p. 318, l. 3). Cf. also *Ḥawādith*, p. 692, ll. 1–4.

[4] Ibn Iyās, iv, p. 329, l. 22, to p. 330, l. 4 ; p. 377, ll. 9–13, 20 ; p. 398,
ll. 1–2.

Dawādār,[1] and sometimes by the vizier (when the holder of this post was an emir and not a native official) [2] ; in Samaria usually by the Grand Dawādār [3] ; in the Beisan plain sometimes by the governor-general of Damascus.[4]

At the time of the Ottoman conquest most of the Egyptian lands became crown domains. This was then the fate of the old domains of the Mamlūk sultans, of the military fiefs, and of all those real estates the owners of which could not produce valid title-deeds.[5] Alexandria, Damietta, Rosetta, and Borollos became a domain of the sultan's palace (*dār al-sa'āda*), and were managed by its agent (*wakīl*) until 1812, when this post was united with that of the deputy (*katkhudā*) of the Egyptian governor-general.[6] The administration of the remaining crown domains, denoted by Ibn Iyās as *al-bilād al-sulṭāniyya* [7] or *aqāṭī' sulṭāniyya*, was conferred upon the Egyptian governor-general, who had to meet from their revenues the cost of the garrison and administration and to pay a yearly tribute to the sultan.[8] During the first seven years after the conquest these domains were exploited through the

---

[1] Ibn Iyās, ii, p. 112, ll. 26–7 ; p. 115, ll. 27–9 ; p. 116, l. 13 ; p. 218, l. 21 ; iv, p. 160, ll. 11–13 ; p. 180, l. 5 ; p. 261, l. 22 ; p. 298, l. 8 ; p. 327, ll. 1–18 ; p. 388, l. 19 ; v, p. 295, l. 20. The rents paid by the farmer of Upper Egypt were fixed for A.H. 871 as 160,000 *irdabbs* of grain in kind, *Ḥawādith*, p. 530, ll. 24–6 (a modern *irdabb* of Cairo is about 198 litres).

[2] Ibn Iyās, ii, p. 215, ll. 11, 17 ; iv, p. 26, l. 5.

[3] Mujīr, pp. 686–7, 694–5, 702. Ibn Iyās, iv, p. 51. The inhabitants of Palestinian towns were forced to purchase at arbitrarily fixed prices the olive-oil levied from the tenants of these domains.

[4] *Ṣubḥ*, iv, p. 183, ll. 17–18 ; p. 188, ll. 6–7 ; p. 190, ll. 19–20. On the identity of *al-aghwār* with the district of Beisan, cf. *Ta'rīf*, p. 178, ll. 15–16 ; *al-a'wār* mentioned in that inscription from Damascus which is referred to by M. Sobernheim, *Das Zuckermonopol unter Sultan Barsbāī* (*Zeitschrift für Assyriologie*, xxvii, 1912), is undoubtedly the same region and not al-Ahwāz or al-Baḥrayn, which never belonged to the Mamlūk state.

[5] Ibn Iyās, v, p. 158, ll. 14–23 ; p. 167, l. 19 ; p. 176, ll. 9–11 ; p. 184, l. 20, to p. 185, l. 16 ; p. 186, ll. 6–15.

[6] Ibid., p. 396, ll. 5–13 ; p. 401, ll. 1–4 ; p. 405, ll. 5–7, 16–18. Jabartī, iii, p. 62, ll. 29–30 ; iv, p. 145, ll. 13–19.

[7] Ibn Iyās, v, p. 403, l. 14.

[8] Ibid., p. 256, ll. 5–7 ; p. 258, ll. 13–15 ; p. 287, ll. 19–21 ; p. 403, l. 2, to p. 405, l. 16.

medium of a small group of experienced officials of the former administration of the Mamlūk crown domains, who were still invested with the honorary titles connected with the departments of the Mamlūk sultan (*nāẓir al-khāṣṣ*, vizier, *ustādār al-'āliya wa-ṣāḥib al-dīwān al-mufrad*, etc.). Every year they divided the crown domains among them; each of them was the chief farmer (*mutaḥaddith 'alā jihāt*) of an entire district (e.g. al-Sharqiyya, al-Gharbiyya, Upper Egypt) and managed it through the medium of local farmers.[1] It was the rebel governor-general, Aḥmad-pasha (1524), who first sought to gain the affection of the military troops through the appointment of their commanders to positions as territorial farmers; his example was imitated by his successors,[2] and this eventually led to the division of the large farmed districts into smaller units. In Syria, Palestine, and the Lebanon we do not find in the sixteenth century fixed and constant rules in regard to the distribution of the crown domains among the farmers and to the conditions of farming. The Jewish farmers of the Tiberias region paid to the crown a considerable sum of money after appointment and a smaller annual tribute [3]—conditions such as we find afterwards in Egypt but not in Palestine; the district governors of " the Turcomans of Aleppo and 'Azāz " and of Manbij and al-Maḍīq were at first, according to 'Ayn-i 'Alī, salaried officials, and afterwards became the chief farmers of their respective districts. Only after the suppression of the revolt of 'Alī Jānbulāṭ, when the farming of the crown domains [4] became

---

[1] Ibid., pp. 158, 185–6, 189, 205–6, 208, 216, 218–19, 263–4, 271–2, 287, 295, 451, 463–4, 488–9. *Taqsīṭ al-bilād* (p. 488, l. 18) = the annual redivision. *'Ummāl al-bilād* or *al-'ummāl* (p. 332, l. 16; p. 445, l. 16; p. 487, l. 22) = the farmers of villages.

[2] Hammer, ii, pp. 37, 38.

[3] De Aveiro, loc. cit.

[4] In Syria and in Palestine these lands are known up to the present day as *mīrī* (*in this case* it is an abbreviation of *arāḍī [a]mīriyya*, " crown domains "), though in practice their legal status hardly differs from that of allodial lands. Prior to the revolt of 'Alī Jānbulāṭ the feudal lands and the crown domains of Syria and Palestine were known collectively as *dīmūz* (" the lands of the community ", from Greek *demos*), or *faṣl*,

the principal form of land tenure in all the countries which
are dealt with in the present survey, there was finally
established that feudal system which existed until the time of
Muḥammad ‘Alī.

This system, which was on general lines a return to the
‘Abbāsid tradition,[1] implied a feudal hierarchy based upon
the payment of an annual tribute by every territorial lord to
his superior. The new *iqtā‘*,[2] called for the most part in
Egypt *iltizām*[3] and in Syria, Palestine, and the Lebanon

mafṣūl (= lands held by the tenants on the condition of *faṣl*, fixed yearly
rents), whereas the allodial lands were designated as *qasm*. The first two
terms described the revenues derived by the lords from " the lands
of the community ", Hammer, ii, p. 344 ; the emir ‘Alī ‘Abd al-‘Azīz
al-Ḥasanī, *Ta’rīkh Sūriyyā al-Iqtiṣādī*, Damascus, A.H. 1342, pp. 149 ff. The
use of the word " *qasm* " instead of the habitual " *mulk* " was probably due
to the fact that the latter term denoted in the Lebanon also those lands
which were included in the crown domains (Shidyāq, p. 112, l. 16, etc.).
As I have shown in *JRAS.*, 1937, p. 98, this custom was brought into the
Lebanon by the terminology of Arabic feudal charters of the Crusaders. In
the ‘Abbāsid and Fāṭimid charters the crown domains held by hereditary
farmers were also sometimes designated as their *mulk* (*Ṣubḥ*, xiii, p. 127,
l. 1 ; p. 132, l. 4 ; p. 141, l. 9), but this designation did not survive in
those parts of the Mamlūk state which remained all the time under the
Moslem rule, and therefore we cannot consider it as the origin of the
Lebanese " *mulk* ".

[1] Cf. Poliak, *La Féodalité Islamique, RÉI.*, 1936, pp. 247-265. The
Ottomans explicitly recognized this similitude, Ibn Iyās, v, p. 122, l. 20.

[2] Jabartī, i, p. 309, l. 20 ; p. 318, l. 10 ; iii, p. 167, l. 8 ; p. 173, l. 15 ;
p. 175, l. 20. Shidyāq, p. 109, l. 17 ; p. 376, l. 6 ; p. 379, l. 6 ; p. 403, l. 12 ;
p. 404, l. 1.

[3] Under the Mamlūks this term meant " the obligation to pay a certain
amount in instalments " (Ibn Iyās, iv, p. 263, l. 8). The verb *iltazama bi* . . .
is still employed in this sense by Ibn Iyās in his accounts of the farmers
of the crown domains after the Ottoman conquest (v, p. 218, l. 21 ;
p. 463, l. 20). Later its meaning was " to farm a crown domain and the
serfs attached to it " (Jabartī, iv, p. 26, l. 31 ; p. 191, l. 29 ; p. 208, ll. 10,
11 ; p. 234, l. 2), and " to farm any source of revenue from the state ".
" The responsibility for the payment of the *mīrī* to the state " was denoted
in Egypt as *dhimma* (Jabartī, i, p. 152, l. 5 ; p. 255, ll. 3–8), and in Syria,
Palestine, and the Lebanon as *‘uhda* (Rustum, i, p. 76, ll. 5–7 ; ii, p. 44,
ll. 3–4 ; p. 45, l. 15). Hence the official appointed in 1810 to control these
payments in Egypt was called *kātib al-dhimma* (Jabartī, iv, p. 108,
ll. 28–9) ; the Lebanese district farmers, *mashā’ikh al-‘uhda* (Michael,
p. 107, l. 14) ; the inhabitants of a farmed district (there, in Syria or in
Palestine), *ahl al-‘uhda* (Rustum, ii, p. 70, l. 5) ; the farmer (of a district
or a village), sometimes, *muta‘ahhid*.

muqāṭaʿa,[1] was not a military fief, since the grant of it was not conditional on the maintenance of a specified contingent of troops, considered as a part of the state army, but on the payment of tribute. The feudatory was, however, entitled to have in his service such armed forces as were necessary for securing the levy of taxes, often utilized them for settling quarrels with his neighbours and for extending the limits of his territory, and was expected to assist his superior with them when the latter was engaged in a similar feud. The weak central government sanctioned most of the changes brought by the use of arms. The province of Egypt was farmed by a collective body, the council (*dīwān*) of the local military commanders, and the governor-general was there only a salaried representative of the central government whose task was to confirm the decisions of the *dīwān*. The most influential member of the *dīwān* was the mayor (*shaykh al-balad*) of Cairo, whom the sources sometimes denote as " the emir of Egypt ".[2]   The *dīwān* farmed all the state revenues (except the domain of the royal palace) and had to meet the cost of the local administration and to send to Constantinople a yearly tribute, *al-khazna* or *al-khazīna*.[3] The local farmer (*multazim*) of a crown domain levied from the peasants the rents of the cultivated lands (*kharāj*), paid to the *dīwān* a fixed tax, the *mīrī*,[4] for every *qīrāṭ* ($= \frac{1}{24}$) of a village, and kept the remainder of the *kharāj*, *al-fāʾiẓ*,[5] for himself.   The *qīrāṭ* was no more a share in the

---

[1] *Recueil de Firmans*, p. 7, No. 22.

[2] Jabartī, i, p. 258, ll. 19–20 ; p. 414, l. 1 ; ii, pp. 151, 261.

[3] Marcel, pp. 195, 244. Jabartī, i, p. 114, ll. 13–14 ; ii, p. 191, l. 6. The emir who convoyed it was designated as *amīr al-khazna* or *ṣanjaq al-khazīna*. On its fluctuations, cf. the introduction to *Recueil de Firmans*.

[4] *Mīrī, māl mīrī, al-mīrī, māl al-mīrī, al-amwāl al-mīriyya, al-māl wa-l-ghilāl al-mīriyya, al-ghilāl wa-l-māl al-mīrī, al-māl wa-l-ghilāl*, Jabartī, i, p. 318, l. 24 ; ii, p. 19, l. 12 ; p. 178, ll. 28–9 ; p. 179, l. 4 ; p. 193, l. 17 ; iii, p. 79, l. 4 ; p. 194, ll. 5, 8, 11–12.

[5] Also *al-fāʾiẓ*, a colloquial form of *al-fāʾiḍ*, Jabartī, i, p. 150, l. 33 ; p. 181, l. 2 ; iii, p. 198, l. 15 ; p. 267, l. 16 ; iv, p. 10, l. 4 ; p. 93, l. 18 ; p. 95, l. 23 ; p. 109, l. 31 ; p. 123, l. 23.

common land of a village (as in the Mamlūk sources) but a
certain piece of land, delimited at the time of the cadastral
survey of 1526.[1] Every *iltizām* was an aggregation of *qīrāṭs*,
which could be portions of various villages ; therefore the
iltizāms were denoted also as " portions ", *ḥiṣaṣ*.[2] The great
iltizāms contained sometimes entire districts,[3] the smallest
only a *qīrāṭ* or half a *qīrāṭ*.[4] In addition to the *mīrī*, the
multazims sometimes farmed extraordinary taxes (*furad* or
furaḏ) imposed on their serfs by the *dīwān*.[5] The military
commanders, if defeated in Cairo by an antagonist party, often
fled to their *iltizāms* in Upper Egypt and transformed this
country into a confederation of independent small rulers
(the so-called " Southern Emirs ", *al-umarā' al-qabālī*), who
sometimes carried on an open war with the authorities of
Cairo and at other times promised to pay the *mīrī* and negotiated
the frontier line with Cairo. Such confederations existed in
1764–7, 1776–7, from 1786 to 1791, and from 1799 to 1811
(with short interruptions). The most influential lord, who
presided over the confederation, was sometimes denoted as
amīr al-Ṣa'īd.[6] In Syria, Palestine, and the Lebanon a province
was usually farmed by the governor-general, who sent to
Constantinople a yearly tribute,[7] met the cost of the local
administration and added the surplus of revenues to his
private fortune. The number of the provinces was raised in
1660 from three (Damascus, Tripoli, Aleppo) to four ; the

---

[1] Marcel, pp. 196–7. Hammer, ii, p. 343. Isḥāqī, p. 136, ll. 3–7. Jabartī,
iv, p. 60, l. 14 ; p. 71, ll. 3–4 ; p. 81, ll. 12–13 ; p. 123, ll. 22–3.

[2] Jabartī, iii, p. 16, l. 19 ; p. 135, l. 14 ; p. 140, l. 1 ; p. 173, l. 30 ;
p. 179, l. 20 ; p. 198, l. 6 ; p. 345, l. 10 ; p. 346, l. 18 ; iv, p. 10, l. 4. Already
in Ibn Iyās, iv, p. 228, l. 19, it is a synonym of *iqṭā'āt*. On the sing. *ḥiṣṣa*,
cf. my note in *JRAS.*, 1937, p. 106.

[3] Jabartī, i, p. 308, l. 17 ; ii, p. 257, l. 31 ; iii, p. 168, ll. 5–6 ; p. 175,
ll. 20–3. Marcel, p. 234.

[4] Jabartī, iv, p. 204, ll. 1–2.

[5] Jabartī, iv, p. 109, ll. 12–18.

[6] Jabartī, iii, p. 82, l. 14 ; p. 106, l. 17 ; p. 192, l. 8. On their negotiations
with Cairo, cf. ii, pp. 154–7, 172–4, 182, 193 ; iii, pp. 228, 345, 351 ;
pp. 89–90, 113.

[7] " *Māl al-irsāliyya* " : Shidyāq, pp. 274–7, 280, 313.

additional province was officially designated as the province of Sidon even after the transfer of the governor-general's seat to Acre (in 1777). Occasionally the post of the chief farmer (*muḥaṣṣil*) was separated from that of the governor-general (e.g. in the province of Aleppo at the time of Volney). The local farmer (*muqāṭaʻajī*) as a rule farmed from the province farmer an entire district. In theory the whole country was divided into fixed districts of this kind (*muqāṭaʻāt*) : e.g. the Lebanon into 24, Judæa and Samaria into 18.[1] In reality the possessions of a *muqāṭaʻajī* sometimes contained several nominal districts, sometimes a part (e.g. a half or a third) of such a district, and in exceptional cases only a village or several villages.[2] The *muqāṭaʻajī* usually exploited his district through the medium of village farmers, who farmed their respective villages from him. Often he paid the *mīrī*[3] not directly to the governor-general but to a man who farmed from the latter a part of the province. Such a farmer was either an Ottoman governor, *mutasallim* (e.g. the governor of Jerusalem at the time of Volney), or the most influential chieftain of a mountainous country dominated by some particular tribe or religious sect (these countries are designated by Volney as *pays abonnés*). Whereas in Egypt the non-agrarian revenues of the state (customs duties, excises, etc.) were usually farmed by particular farmers, in Syria, Palestine, and the Lebanon they were for the most part levied through the medium of the *muqāṭaʻajīs*.[4]

The *mīrī* levied by the provincial farmer from the local

---

[1] Shidyāq, pp. 19–33. *PEFQS.*, 1905, pp. 352–6.

[2] Shidyāq, p. 30, ll. 1–2 ; p. 90, l. 8 ; p. 105, ll. 14–15 ; p. 137, ll. 2–3 ; p. 145*b*, ll. 15–16. The charters collected by Rustum (i, pp. 121–3 ; ii, pp. 24–6, 53–4, 59–60, 69–71).

[3] *Al-māl al-amīrī* (Shidyāq, pp. 360, 361, 366, 370), *al-amwāl al-amīriyya* (ibid., pp. 111–13), *al-māl al-sulṭānī* (ibid., pp. 189, 290, 293, 339, 372, 381), *māl al-mīrī* (Michael, pp. 64, 67, 75), *amwāl al-mīrī* (ibid., pp. 25, 106), *al-mīrī* (ibid., pp. 74, 94).

[4] Volney, i, pp. 202, 204 ;' ii, pp. 128–9, 154, 167, 232, 332–3. ii, pp. 24–6.

farmers were as a rule but a small portion of the rents collected by the latter : in the province of Sidon at the end of the eighteenth century about a one-twentieth ; in Egypt from 40 to 4 per cent of the nominal *kharāj*, according to local custom.[1] Particularly favoured local farmers were wholly or partly exempt from the *mīrī*. In Egypt such estates were denoted as *khazīnat band*, and the permanent exemption could be granted only by a royal rescript; in Syria, Palestine, and the Lebanon it could be granted also by a superior farmer (a governor-general, the emir of the Lebanon), but then it involved an increase of the *mīrī* paid by the neighbour local farmers.[2] In Syria and in Palestine the estates held by the governors-general and soldiers were also sometimes exempt from the *mīrī* (and denoted respectively as *arpaliqs* and *tīmārs*) ; in the latter case, however, the exemption lasted only until the death of the holder, and in the first it meant that this estate was not brought into account when the tribute due from his holder was fixed.[3]

In theory every man of wealth could become a farmer, and there was among the farmers a non-Moslem minority : Copts in Egypt,[4] Jews in Palestine,[5] Christian tribal chieftains [6] in the Lebanon. Most of the farmers belonged, however, to the military, tribal, or religious nobility.

(*a*) During the first years after the conquest the Ottoman

---

[1] W. G. Browne (visited Acre in 1797), cited in *PEFQS.*, 1906, p. 137. Lancret, *Mémoire sur le système d'imposition territoriale* (*Description de l'Égypte, État Moderne*, i), p. 254.

[2] Jabartī, iv, p. 94, ll. 14–17. Rustum, i, p. 23. Shidyāq, pp. 90, 104, 110, 112, 701.

[3] Rustum, i, pp. 36–7. Volney, ii, pp. 167, 374. Kiātib Chalabī, *Jihānnumā*, p. 587.

[4] Jabartī, iii, p. 345, l. 10.

On the eighteenth century, cf. Y. Nabon, *Nehpa ba-Kesef*, Jerusalem A.M. 5603, ii, 55a. The banker family of Farhī, whose members had considerable influence on the economical and political life of the provinces of Damascus and Acre in the first half of the nineteenth century, held many villages : Michael, p. 47, ll. 8–9.

[6] Mostly Maronites, but the al-'Āzars were members of the Greek Church (Shidyāq, p. 19, l. 10).

troops stationed in Egypt were prevented from intermarrying with the natives, and often a part of them was replaced by fresh forces from Turkey.[1] Sulaymān the Magnificent stabilized the local garrison, which consisted since that time of seven regiments[2] : (1) *mutafarriqa*, the guard ; (2) *chāwushiyya* or *jāwishiyya*, the tax-collectors ; (3) *jamalyān* (*gamulyān*) or *gönüllü*, the camel regiment ; (4) *tufchiyya*, *tufakjiyān*, or *tufakchiyya*, the gunners ; (5) *charākisa*, the former mamlūk (Circassian) troops[3] ; (6) *yankijariyya*, *inkishāriyya*, or *mustahfizān*,[4] the janissaries ; (7) *'azab*, the footmen. The second, third, and fourth regiments were considered as *sipāhīs* (*isbāhiyya*, *isbahāniyya*), viz. free soldiers hired by the sultan, and the janissaries as his slaves.[5] The seven regiments gradually became a hereditary corporation of civilian artisans, merchants, and pensioners, who received a fixed allowance in money (*jāmakiyya*) and in grain (*jarayāt*, *ghilāl al-anbār*, *ghilāl al-shuwan*). The right to receive this allowance could be sold and dedicated as endowment to some pious purpose.[6] The money and grain were derived from the *mīrī* collected by the *dīwān*, and were distributed through the medium of " the elders " (*ikhtiyāriyya*) of every regiment, who were represented in the *dīwān*.[7] The real infantry in the *dīwān*'s service consisted of foreign mercenaries (and sometimes

---

[1] Ibn Iyās, v, pp. 229–230, 233–5, 251–2, 405, 446–7.

[2] Marcel, pp. 192–4. Hammer, i, p. 377 ; ii, pp. 343, 724. Jabartī, i, pp. 31, 34, 37, 39, 45, 46, 50, 58, 59, 60, 62, 92, 95 ; ii, pp. 150, 182, 188, etc. The term " regiment " is rendered by Jabartī as *tā'ifa*, *buluk*, or *wijāq* (an Arabized form of *ojāq*).

[3] Their contingent was diminished for fiscal reasons in 1522 (Ibn Iyās, v, pp. 448, 453), and as punishment for their revolts in 1523 and 1524.

[4] The term *mustahfizān* is misunderstood by M. van Berchem in *JA.*, 8e sér., xviii, p. 60.

[5] Cf. Ibn Iyās, v, p. 362, l. 6, and Jabartī, i, p. 34, l. 2 ; p. 50, l. 19 ; p. 95, ll. 16–17, etc.

[6] Jabartī, i, p. 37, ll. 1–4 ; ii, p. 258, l. 33 ; iii, p. 212, l. 18, to p. 213, l. 13 (the members were denoted collectively as *ashāb al-'atāmina*, " the recipients of aspers ", i, p. 148, l. 3). Volney, i, p. 151.

[7] Jabartī, i, p. 253, ll. 11–12 ; ii, p. 105, l. 29 ; p. 258, l. 33 ; iii, p. 212, l. 21. Marcel, pp. 193–4.

temporarily mobilized peasants),[1] whose social position was very humble ; the real cavalry—of the new mamlūk corps. The members of this corps were the only real knights, and only they were entitled to mount horses within the boundaries of the Egyptian towns.[2] Their commanders, whose titular number was twenty-four,[3] received at the time of their investiture (as higher military commanders in other parts of the Empire) a flag (rank, ghāya) and a drum (tabl),[4] and therefore they were designated as sanjāq-beys [5] or ṭablakhāna-beys.[6] A commander was not obliged to farm an iltizām of specified size or to have in his service a specified number of mamlūks, but he was esteemed in direct proportion to the size of the former and to the number of the latter.[7] The question of awlād al-nās existed no more, because most of the mamlūks' children died now in the first years of their life [8] ; therefore the possessions of the commanders were usually inherited by their mamlūks.[9] The common mamlūks,[10]

---

[1] Jabartī, i, p. 148, ll. 2–4 ; p. 335, l. 26 ; p. 350, l. 32 ; p. 364, l. 31.

[2] Volney, i, p. 153. At the end of the eighteenth century their number was 8,500–10,000 (ibid., p. 151 ; Jabartī, iv, p. 113, ll. 25–6).

[3] Jabartī, i, p. 58, ll. 21–3 ; Marcel, pp. 193–5. It included several dignitaries sent from Constantinople for a year. The real number was often considerably smaller, especially after the French conquest.

[4] Jabartī, i, p. 32, l. 33, to p. 33, l. 3 ; p. 100, l. 21. Cf. al-būq wa-l-'alam of the Mamlūk epoch.

[5] Instead of sanjāq-bey (" the emir of flag "), Jabartī usually writes ṣanjaq (plur. ṣanājiq), and the European sources " bey " (cf. Marcel, p. 193). The term " emirs " is applied by Jabartī (ii, p. 2, ll. 3–8 ; p. 150, l. 20 ; p. 188, ll. 20–1, etc.), also to " the elders " of the seven regiments, as aghā (colonel), katkhudā (second-in-command), jāwīsh (revenue-collector), etc.

[6] Jabartī, i, p. 32, l. 33, to p. 33, l. 3 (ṣāḥib ṭablakhāna) ; Sulūk, i, pp. 173–4, n. 54.

[7] Jabartī, iv, p. 27, ll. 10–12.

[8] Exaggerated by Volney, i, p. 99 (tous leurs enfans périssent dans le premier ou le second âge). The reason probably lies in the enormous diffusion of syphilis among the mamlūks since the end of the fifteenth century (Ibn Iyās, ii, pp. 344, 373 ; iv, p. 460, ll. 3–7 ; Volney, i, p. 224).

[9] Jabartī, i, p. 139, l. 18 ; p. 318, ll. 10–11 ; ii, p. 257, l. 11 ; iii, p. 140, ll. 25–6.

[10] They were denoted as mamālīk or al-ghuzz (Jabartī, i, p. 346, l. 28 ; p. 348, l. 5 ; cf. my note on this term in RÉI., 1935, p. 237) ; those of

as the private mamlūks of the Mamlūk epoch, were as a rule
foreigners (and particularly Caucasians), and during their
military education they were slaves of their lords.[1] All
the commanders and a considerable portion of the common
mamlūks were *multazims*.[2] Many *iltizāms* were held by wives
and widows of emirs and knights,[3] because the person
and possessions of a woman were inviolable even when the
male members of her family were outlawed. In Syria and
in Palestine the Ottoman garrisons (mostly the janissaries)
also gradually became a hereditary corporation of pacific
pensioners,[4] who sometimes held lands as *tīmārs* ; the district
muqāṭa'ajī often levied on these estates a tax, lighter than the
usual *mīrī*.[5] There was no new permanent corps of cavalry
(as the new mamlūks in Egypt), and those irregular horsemen
who were in the service of the farmers were mercenaries.[6]
In the sixteenth century the government used to bestow upon
a governor-general the military title of *baylarbay*,[7] and upon
a district governor—that of *sanjāq*-bey or *mīr-i liwā'*, even
when he was not a military fief-holder but a salaried official
or a farmer.[8] This custom remained during the greater part of
the seventeenth century [9] ; afterwards the Ottoman governors-

them who were in the service of a commander on the same terms as other
mamlūks without being his freedmen (like *mustakhdamūn* of the Mamlūk
epoch)—as *atbā'*.

[1] Volney, i, pp. 89, 95, 151, 166. The *atbā'* were now usually freedmen
of late commanders.

[2] Volney, i, p. 172 ; Jabartī, iii, p. 267, l. 16 ; iv, p. 113, l. 27, etc.

[3] Jabartī, iii, p. 140, l. 12 ; p. 346, ll. 18–19 ; p. 347, l. 4 ; iv, p. 93, ll. 1–4 ;
p. 204.

[4] Volney, ii, p. 131.

[5] Rustum, ii, pp. 25–6.

[6] Shidyāq, p. 273, l. 13 ; p. 318, l. 2 (the cavalry of Fakhr al-Dīn II
amounted in 1613–14 to less than 500 horses : Mariti, p. 168). Volney, ii,
pp. 132–3, 334 (the total number was at his time 3,400).

[7] Under the Mamlūks it belonged in Cairo to the generalissimo (Ẓāhirī,
p. 112, l. 22), but the title *malik al-umarā'* (held by governors-general)
was possibly also a translation of it.

[8] Belin therefore includes these governors in the total number of the
feudal troops, but it is not exact.

[9] Roque, p. 106. Shidyāq, p. 255, l. 14 ;
p. 275, l. 14, etc.

general and governors received civilian titles (*wazīr*, *muta-sallim*), and the tribal chieftains only the titles particular to them.[1]

(*b*) All the Lebanese farmers, a considerable portion of the Syro-Palestinian, and a smaller of the Egyptian were tribal chieftains. The ruling family of the Lebanon were between 1516–1697 the Ma'n emirs,[2] between 1697–1841 the Shihāb emirs, and between 1842–1861 the Arslān emirs (in the South) and the Abū l-Lam' emirs (in the North). The official position of the Lebanon was that of a *pays abonné*, the ruler of which farmed it at first from the governor-general of Damascus (between 1624–1633 directly from the sultan), and later from that of Sidon. The Northern Lebanon was usually included in the province of Tripoli and administered by a representative of the Lebanese emir (from 1617 to 1635 a member of the al-Khāzin family, from 1636 to 1763 mostly one of the Ḥamāda family, from 1763 to 1790 a member of the Shihāb family), who was a vassal of the governor-general of Tripoli and of the emir at the same time.[3] The emirs Fakhr al-Dīn II (1598–1634) and Bashīr II (1788–1840) sought to transform the Lebanon into a centralized state, where the emir was the only owner of the soil [4] and could divide and redivide it among the district farmers and tenants according to his own desire. The normal state of things was, however, that the emir had

---

[1] Prior to 1855, no Lebanese Christian was constituted bey (Shidyāq, p. 187), though there were among them two families of emirs (the Ballama's, the Christianized Shihābs). It was an exceptional honour for a tribal chieftain to become even a common member of an Ottoman regiment (p. 222, l. 9 ; p. 688, ll. 3–4).

[2] The emirs of Āl Tanūkh ruled till 1603 independently of them al-Gharb and the eastern slopes of the Lebanon. Ibn Firāq and Sharaf al-Dīn, mentioned by Minadoi (utilized by Mariti, pp. 63–81, and by Hammer, ii, pp. 530–1), are two emirs of Āl Tanūkh, Muḥammad and Mundhir (Shidyāq, pp. 246, 252, 677). Kasrawān was ruled until 1590 by a Turcoman family, the 'Assāf emirs.

[3] Volney, ii, pp. 14–15, 154–5. F. von Olberg, *Geschichte des Krieges zwischen Mehemed Ali und der Ottomanischen Pforte*, Berlin, 1837, p. 37. For particulars, cf. Shidyāq.

[4] Mariti, p. 165. Michael, p. 102, ll. 9–16.

to address every *muqāṭa'ajī* in his letters as " dear brother ",[1] as he was himself practically but one of them (Shidyāq considers the Shihāb emirs as the lords of the Beirut district), owed his superior position to their election,[2] and only their own consent or the pressure of rival neighbours obliged them to comply with his demands. The principal Druse families of *muqāṭa'ajīs* were the Arslāns, lords of the lower al-Gharb ; the Jānbulāṭs, lords of al-Shūf, Jazzīn, al-Tuffāḥ, al-Kharrūb, and Jabal al-Rayḥān [3] ; the Talḥūqs, lords of the upper al-Gharb since 1711 ; the Nakads, lords of al-Shaḥḥār and al-Manāṣif ; the 'Amāds, lords of al-'Urqūb (chiefs of the Yazbakī confederation, which included the Talḥūqs and 'Abd al-Maliks) ; the 'Abd al-Maliks, lords of al-Jurd since 1711. The principal Christian : the Abū l-Lam's (Ballama's), lords of al-Qāṭi', al-Matn, and al-Shūf al-Bayāḍī ; the al-Khāzins, lords of Kasrawān since 1613 (the oldest Christian *muqāṭa'ajīs*) ; the Hubayshes, lords of Ghazīr since 1680 ; the al-Ẓāhirs, lords of al-Zāwiya since the end of the seventeenth century ; the al-Daḥdāḥs, lords of al-Futūḥ since 1704 ; the Abū Ṣa'bs, lords of al-Quwayṭi' since 1753 ; the al-'Āzars, lords of the upper al-Kūra. The Sunnis were represented by the Kurdish emirs of the village Rās Naḥāsh, and the Shi'ītes by the Ḥamādas, lords of Jabbat Munayẓira and adjacent regions.[4] According to Shidyāq, the Arslāns traced their genealogy back to the pre-Islamic Arab kings of al-Ḥīra [5] ; the Shihābs to a Qurayshi Companion of Muḥammad, al-Ḥārith

---

[1] Shidyāq, pp. 89, 104, 145*b*, 157*b*, 160*b*, 174, 366.

[2] Mariti, p. 94. Shidyāq, pp. 358–9, 378–9, 386.

[3] The former lords of Killis, who emigrated to the Lebanon in 1630.

[4] The principal sources on the Lebanese feudal families are hitherto Shidyāq and *Ta'rīkh* of the emir Ḥaydar Shihāb (ed. 1900). Cf. also I. Aouad, *Le droit privé des Maronites au temps des émirs Chihab*, Paris, 1933, and the discussion of Q. al-Bāshā and N. S. al-Daḥdāḥ in *Ma.*, 1935–6.

[5] The same descent was formerly claimed by Āl Tanūkh (Ibn Yaḥyā, pp. 44–8), and by the Ramtūnī chieftains (Ibn Ḥajar, i, p. 541). B. Abī l-Jaysh of the Mamlūk epoch considered themselves as descendants of the bedouin tribe, al-Ḥammīrā, in the plain of al-Biqā' (Ibn Yaḥyā, p. 47, ll. 9–11).

b. Hishām ; the Talhūqs and Nakads to the twelfth century ;
the al-Dahdāhs to the fourteenth ;   the Hamādas to the
fifteenth ;   the Jānbulāts, Hubayshes, al-Khāzins, and the
emirs of Rās Nahāsh to the sixteenth ; the Abū Saʿbs, ʿAmāds,
and Ballamaʿs to the seventeenth ;   the al-Zāhirs and ʿAbd
al-Maliks to the eighteenth.   At the end of the eighteenth
century about one-tenth of the Lebanese lands was held
directly by the *muqātaʿajīs* [1] as their estates (*arzāq, ʿaqārāt*),
often committed to managers [2] ;   the remainder was held
by their vassals,[3] viz. the hereditary farmers of villages,
and by Christian monasteries and churches.[4] The hereditary titles of nobility were bestowed by the emir of the
Lebanon,[5] and were connected with the land tenure : he
who was appointed the farmer of a village became a *muqaddam*
or a *shaykh*, the *muqātaʿajī* was a *shaykh* or an emir.[6] The noblemen as a whole (*manāsib, aʿyān, wujūh*) used to ride horses
when they commanded their peasant troops during hos-
tilities, and to intermarry only with noble families.[7] There
were also families of *khaddāmūn*, hereditary professional
soldiers in the service of noble lords, who received a fixed
pay (*nafʿ*).[8]

In other *pays abonnés* the social structure resembled that
of the Lebanon but was less elaborated. In two of them the
rulers succeeded in becoming the exclusive lords of the soil :

[1] Volney, ii, pp. 58–9.

[2] *Arzāq*, Shidyāq, pp. 113, 146, 190, 567 ;   Michael, pp. 76, 106, 107.
The Hamādas used to denote theirs as *bakālīk*, sing. *baklīk* (" a domain of
bey "), Shidyāq, p. 167, ll. 2, 4. *ʿAqārāt*, ibid., pp. 110, 186, 683. The.
manager was denoted as *dihqān* (ibid., pp. 68, 81, 186, 347), or *shūbāsī*
(Michael, p. 90, l. 22), and must not be confounded with *mudabbir*, the
prime minister of a feudal lord.

[3] *Atbāʿ, tibaʿ* : Michael, p. 79, l. 12 ;   p. 107, l. 15.

[4] Shidyāq, pp. 137, 190. *PEFQS.*, 1891, p. 104.

[5] Shidyāq, p. 365, ll. 13, 21.   The *shaykhs* and *muqaddams* could be
dubbed also by the *muqātaʿajīs* : p. 377, l. 21.

[6] Ibid., pp. 67, 109, 112, 157*b*, 160*b*, 187, etc.

[7] This custom existed already under the Mamlūks, Ibn Yahyā, p. 165,
ll. 5–6.

[8] Michael, p. 108, ll. 19–20

in (1) the modern Jabal al-Durūz, ruled by the Ḥamdān family from 1685 to 1869 (at first as vassals of the Lebanese emir), and by the al-Aṭrash family since 1869,[1] and in (2) Bilād Ḥāritha (Mount Carmel and the adjacent region in the south), ruled until the sixties of the seventeenth century by a bedouin family, Āl Ṭarābāy, *sanjāq*-beys of al-Lujūn.[2] The al-Ḥarfūsh emirs, Shī'ite lords of Baalbek and the plain of al-Biqā',[3] and the Zaydān *shaykhs*, bedouin lords of Galilee during the first three-quarters of the eighteenth century,[4] occupied in their respective areas, a place similar to that of the Lebanese emir, of whom they were not infrequently vassals. The land of the Nuṣayrīs ('Alawīs) was divided among several chieftains (*muqaddamūn*), who paid the *mīrī* to the governor-general of Tripoli. Samaria (Jabal Nābulus) was divided among several *shaykhs* ; sometimes one of them was appointed the chief farmer, and sometimes they held this post as a body.[5] At least one of these families, al-Jayyūsī (lords of the B. Ṣa'b region), is mentioned already in a Mamlūk source[6] ; but the 'Abd al-Hādīs and al-Jarrārs, between whom the al-Sha'rawiyya region was divided, and the Tūqāns, lords of the town of Nablus, gradually became more prominent. In other parts of Syria and Palestine[7] the tribal chieftains were numerous among the farmers of villages and districts, and exceptionally attained for a short time even

---

[1] Bouron, p. 333.

[2] Roque, pp. 106, 108–9, 157. On the history of Āl Ṭarābāy, cf. Ibn Iyās, v, pp. 290, 320–1, 370 ; Mariti, pp. 221, 243, 248, 265 ; Roque, pp. 103–4, 261–2 ; Shidyāq, pp. 55, 136, 253, 259, 279, 287, 296, 304–5, 315, 318–323, 335–6, 357, 676 ; *ZDPV.*, xxx, 1907, p. 146 ; xxxi, 1908, p. 62 (the emir's name in the inscription is 'Assāf b. Timur bāy).

[3] Ibn Iyās, v, p. 248. Mariti, pp. 64–75, 116, 308. Hammer, ii, pp. 530–1. Volney, ii, pp. 80–3. Shidyāq (many times). Michael, pp. 74, 79, 89, 90.

[4] Shidyāq, pp. 360–1, 394–5, 398 ; Mariti, p. 315, and other sources.

[5] Rustum, i, pp. 75–6. Michael, pp. 16, 63, 71, 72. Shidyāq p. 382. Finn, i, p. 239.

[6] Ibn Iyās, iv, p. 193, ll. 7–8.

[7] Cf. the lists of Palestinian tribal feudatories in *PEFQS.*, 1905, pp. 352–6, and *JPOS.*, 1929, pp. 73–4.

the rank of governors-general [1] ; their position was, however, very precarious in comparison with the *pays abonnés*. In Egypt a tribal chieftain was denoted as *shaykh al-'arab*,[2] even if his origin was not bedouin but peasant. He was a *multazim*, and at the same time a *ṣāḥib al-darak*, viz. the protector of caravans and ships which passed through his sphere of influence. In 1769–1770 the mamlūk *shaykh al-balad*, 'Alī bey, destroyed the power of the strongest among them : the emir Hammām of the Hawwāra tribe in Upper Egypt and the Ḥabīb *shaykhs* (of rural stock), in al-Qalyūbiyya.[3]

(c) The spiritual nobility consisted of the hereditary managers of *waqfs*, recipients of their revenues and holders of Moslem religious offices. Their social position was now much higher than in the Mamlūk state : the *siyāsa* existed no more, and at least in the towns the *qāḍīs* and *muftīs* had judicial authority over the whole Moslem population (the rural population had manorial and tribal courts of justice) ; the religious administration was then more separated from the general, and its local chiefs were usually hereditary [4] ; the number of learned men was also much smaller, and the members of these families were therefore employed in the civil service even more than before. In a relatively small town such as Jerusalem they " form the aristocracy ", " intermarry exclusively with each other, and must be carefully distinguished by us from the few transient Turkish officials, who form technically ' the government ', and are helpless in effective administration against or without the local knowledge and corporate union " of these families.[5] But even in Cairo this

---

[1] e.g. a member of a Kurdish family, B. Sayfā, was from 1579 to 1619 the governor-general of Tripoli (Shidyāq, pp. 350–3).

[2] Jabartī, i, pp. 52, 181, 318, 336, 342, 344, 345.

[3] Jabartī, i, pp. 342–9. Marcel, p. 234. Volney, i, p. 111. On *aṣḥāb al-darak*, cf. Jabartī, i, p. 348, l. 25.

[4] Volney, ii, p. 371.

[5] Finn, i, p. 180. They were collectively denoted there (not in Egypt !) as effendis (sing. *afandī* = " Mr."), which was then the official title of Moslem government clerks (cf. Marcel, pp. 194–5 ; Jabartī, i, p. 53, l. 32 ; ii, p. 176, l. 21 ; iii, p. 267, l. 13 ; iv, p. 123, l. 21.)

nobility was second in rank to the mamlūks only, and held
a considerable part of the Egyptian *iltizāms*.[1] In addition
to the *waqfs*, they supervised also *al-rizaq al-aḥbāsiyya*, the
extent of which in Egypt continued to grow, owing to
additional endowments by the sultans and *multazims* (who
set apart for this purpose portions of their demesne lands),
so that at the commencement of the nineteenth century this
category of lands was the principal one in Upper Egypt and
amounted there to 600,000 *faddāns*.[2] When the mamlūks
were driven out of Lower Egypt by the French troops in
1798, the spiritual " *shaykhs* " became the uppermost class
of the native society. The new *dīwān* consisted at first of
their representatives only, instead of the military, and the
French constitutional theory of that time (the government
must be vested in the most learned and experienced men,
" the elders ") served as juridic reason for that change.[3]

To recapitulate : in the *pays abonnés* the farmers were
tribal chieftains ; in Egypt military, spiritual, and tribal
noblemen (all of them permanent residents of the country) ;
in those parts of Syria and Palestine which were under the
direct Ottoman rule—partly native noblemen, and partly
Turkish officials,[4] usually sent thither for a very short time
(the governors-general were appointed for one year). The
character of the land tenure differed accordingly. In the
Lebanon at the time of Volney it was practically private
property, " sacred as in Europe." [5] The Egyptian *iltizām*
was a lifelong possession, which the farmer could alienate
by sale, mortgage, and lease out.[6] In the event of his death

---

[1] Jabartī, iii, p. 61, l. 14 ; p. 166, l. 19 ; p. 210, l. 9 ; iv, p. 88, l. 3 ;
p. 188, ll. 16–17 ; p. 234. Volney, i, pp. 172, 188.

[2] Jabartī, iv, p. 93, l. 18, to p. 95, l. 5 ; p. 123, l. 33, to p. 124, l. 2 ;
p. 141, l. 32 ; p. 209, ll. 31–2.

[3] Al-Sharqāwī, *Tuḥfat al-Nāḍirīn* (written in 1801), printed with Isḥāqī,
p. 154. Jabartī, iii, p. 5, ll. 4–8, etc. Hence the term *mashyakha*, employed
by the French authorities as a translation of " republic ".

[4] *Recueil de Firmans*, p. 7. *JA.*, 6e sér., iv (1864), p. 351.

[5] Volney, ii, pp. 17, 369.

[6] " Alienation " *fighār* (Jabartī, i, p. 181, ll. 27–32), or *nuzūl* (p. 305,
l. 14) ; " mortgage " *rahn* (p. 181, l. 26) ; " lease " *ūjār* (p. 181, ll. 1, 13).

his sons and mamlūks had the right of priority to farm it[1] ;
otherwise it was considered as vacant (*maḥlūl*),[2] and the new
farmer had to pay to the authorities its price, *ḥulwān*,[3]
fixed by public competition, *mazād*.[4] In "the Ottoman"
parts of Syria and Palestine the crown domains were farmed
for one year only, and the farmers used therefore to exploit
their serfs in a most cruel manner. The remedy proposed
by the Imperial Government[5] was the *mālikāna* (Turk.
pronunc. *malikiane*), a Turkish system similar to the Egyptian
iltizām. The efforts to introduce it were, however, unsuccessful,
as the Imperial Government could not sufficiently protect
these estates, neither from the powerful tribal chieftains[6]
nor from the governors-general themselves, for whom the
annual local farming was the best means for deriving the
maximum of money from the province during their own
short term of service. In Egypt small *iltizāms* were also
often seized by their powerful neighbours,[7] but on the whole
the land tenure was relatively stable there, and many lands
remained allodial.[8] In "the Ottoman" parts of Syria and
Palestine all the allodial lands which were not within the
boundaries of inhabited places or on their outskirts were
gradually annexed to the crown domains, from which the
governors derived greater revenue.[9] Owing to the perpetually
disturbed conditions, for the Syro-Palestinian governors-
general every annual collection of the *mīrī* was a military

---

[1] Ibid., iii, p. 140, ll. 25–6. *Recueil*, p. 7, No. 22. The heirs had to pay
a fee fixed by the *dīwān*.

[2] Jabartī, i, pp. 99, 139, 206 ; iii, pp. 198, 251, 267 ; iv, pp. 94, 256.

[3] Ibid., i, p. 99, l. 33 ; p. 150, l. 25 ; p. 184, l. 10 ; p. 206, l. 6. Ibn
Iyās, iv, p. 283, l. 4, denotes so the payment levied in A.H. 918 by the
sultan from emirs for the *otlīq* lands.

[4] Jabartī, ii, pp. 152–3 ; iii, pp. 198, 288, 345, 346.

[5] Cf. Belin in *JA.*, 6ᵉ sér., iv (1864), pp. 351–3.

[6] Cf. Michael, pp. 25, 44, 91–2, 94, on the plain of al-Biqā'.

[7] *Recueil*, p. 3, Nos. 5, 6 ; p. 11, No. 38. Jabartī, ii, p. 257, ll. 31–2 ;
iv, p. 64, ll. 3–11.

[8] In 1878 they amounted to 1,323,000 acres (Cromer, p. 89).

[9] Volney, ii, p. 369. Rustum, iii–iv, p. 65, l. 14. *PEFQS.*, 1894, p. 191.

expedition,[1] and the rival native feudatories were organized in hereditary factions (the members of which could, however, pass from one to another) : the Faqārī and the Qāsimī among the Egyptian military nobility, Niṣf Saʻd and Niṣf Ḥarām among the Egyptian tribesmen, the Qaysī and the Yamanī among the Syro-Palestinian and Lebanese tribal chieftains, the Jānbulāṭī and the Yazbakī among the Lebanese.[2]

---

[1] *Dawra* (" round ") : Jabartī, iv, p. 266, ll. 20–6 ; Michael, p. 73, l. 91.

[2] On Egypt, cf. Marcel, p. 221 ; Jabartī, i, pp. 21–4, 52, 63–4, 318. The Qays-Yaman rivalry existed under the Mamlūks only among the peasants, whereas the nomads were considered as Yamanīs, *Sulūk*, I, i, p. 186, n. 65 ; *Taʻrīf*, p. 113 ; *Ṣubḥ*, iv, pp. 203–215 ; xii, p. 324.

V. Serfdom

Under all the feudal systems which we have described
the peasants were serfs of their immediate lords.[1] The serf
could not leave his village without permission of his lord,
and then only for a specified time ; otherwise the lord could
bring him back with assistance of the authorities, and was
even obliged by them to do so.[2] The lord could punish his
serf with flogging and jail,[3] and sometimes even put him to
death.[4] He was entitled to decide civil lawsuits among his
serfs, if the suitors preferred him to the *qāḍī* or to an arbiter.[5]
The serf could not submit a plaint against his lord to legal
or administrative authorities. When in 1521 the Egyptian
governor-general was asked by the peasants of a *rizqa* to
compel their lord to levy from them more reasonable rents,
and gave orders to this effect, the lord replied that nobody
is entitled to interpose himself between him and his serfs,
and the final victory was his.[6] The lord, on the contrary,

---

[1] The technical terms are : " serfdom " *falāḥa* (*Khiṭaṭ*, i, p. 85, l. 37) ;
" serf " *fallāḥ* (ibid., ll. 37–8 ; *Nujūm*, vii, p. 93, l. 15 ; Jabartī, iv, p. 109,
l. 14 ; p. 130, l. 21 ; p. 207, ll. 13 ff.), sometimes with the addition " attached
to the soil " *qarārī* (Nuwayrī, viii, p. 248, l. 11), or *qarrār* (*Khiṭaṭ*, i, p. 85,
l. 38) ; " lord " *ustādh* (*Nujūm*, vii, p. 93, l. 18 ; *Ḥawādith*, p. 654, l. 9 ;
Manhal, ii, f. 94 ; Jabartī, i, p. 349, l. 15 ; ii, p. 240, l. 6 ; iv, p. 207,
ll. 16, 22 ; p. 208, ll. 1, 7), or *sayyid* (Jabartī, iii, p. 294, l. 31).

[2] Ibn Iyās, iv, p. 104, l. 18. Nuwayrī, viii, p. 298, l. 7. Jabartī, ii, p. 115,
ll. 30–1 ; iii, p. 294, ll. 30–1 ; iv, p. 81, l. 22 ; p. 207, ll. 15–17. Rustum
(*advance notice*, 1928), p. 12.

[3] Ibn Iyās, v, p. 372, l. 22, to p. 373, l. 1. Jabartī, iv, p. 68, l. 28 ; p. 191,
l. 30 ; p. 207, ll. 19, 31, 33 ; p. 208, l. 1.

[4] Ibn Iyās, iv, p. 125, ll. 6–8 (in A.H. 913, a legal punishment). Jabartī, i,
p. 180, l. 25 (in A.H. 1149, possibly an illegal action). Especially in the
pays abonnés, where the lord was at the same time the tribal chieftain.

[5] Jabartī, iv, p. 207, l. 28, to p. 208, l. 3. Rustum, i, p. 76, ll. 7–8. On
the history of tribal courts of justice, cf. el-Barghuthi, *Judicial Courts
among the Bedouin of Palestine* (*JPOS.*, 1922, pp. 34–65), and the articles
published in *Ma.*, 1933, by W. Khūrī (*al-Qaḍā' fī Lubnān 'alā 'Ahd al-Ḥukm
al-Iqṭā'ī*), and I. A. Ma'lūf (*al-Qaḍā' fī Lubnān bi-Zaman al-Umarā' al-
Shihābiyyīn*).

[6] Ibn Iyās, v, p. 395, l. 10, to p. 396, l. 3 ;

could demand the authorities to punish his serf, if he had no means of doing it himself. Under the Mamlūks he had in this case to bring the serf before a military judge, *ḥājib*.[1]

The servile tenants paid to the lord the rents of the cultivated lands, *kharāj*,[2] levied on the lands considered by Islamic law as " tithe-paying " as well as on those regarded by it as " tribute-paying ".[3] In Syria, Palestine, and the Lebanon these rents were a fixed share (*muqāsama*) of the produce : under the Mamlūks mostly one-third or one-quarter, in irrigated lands one-half, in newly colonized one-fifth or one-sixth, in those exposed to assaults of an enemy (including the villages near the sea-coast, not infrequently ravaged by European corsairs), one-seventh or one-eighth. The rents of the arable lands were levied in grain ; of the fruit trees and vegetables, in money ; of the olive groves, in olive oil ; of the mulberry trees, in silk ; of the pomegranates, in fruit-stones, employed then both for food and medicine.[4] We know that in the regions conquered from the Franks (and probably also in those captured from the Ayyūbids), the Mamlūks at first accepted without changes the taxation usual under the former rulers ; the uniform system could emerge but gradually, and its definitive form dates probably from 1313.[5] After the Ottoman conquest, as we learn from the provincial fiscal codes (*qānūn-nāma*)

---

[1] *Nujūm,* vii, p. 267, l. 15, to p. 268, l. 1 (on a particularly humane judge, who, having no legal power to decide the cases to the benefit of the serfs, implored the lords to be more just to them).

[2] Nuwayrī, viii, p. 245, ll. 8 ff. *Khiṭaṭ,* i, p. 103, ll. 22 ff. *Ṣubḥ,* iii, p. 452, ll. 14 ff. *Nujūm,* vi, p. 69, ll. 9–10. Jabartī, ii, p. 109, l. 5 ; iii, p. 194, ll. 8, 12 ; iv, p. 208, l. 10 ; p. 209, l. 2 ; p. 293, l. 3. Also *ray'* (Nuwayrī, viii, p. 258, l. 4), *mughall* (*Khiṭaṭ,* i, p. 90, l. 17), *shūbṣa* (Michael, p. 47, l. 8).

[3] *Ḥawādiṯh,* p. 126, l. 14, to p. 127, l. 3. Ibn Yaḥyā, p. 102, l. 13, to p. 103, l. 1.

[4] Nuwayrī, viii, pp. 258–261. Ibn Yaḥyā, p. 181, ll. 3–4. Mujīr, pp. 686–7, 694–5, 702. Anonym, p. 81, ll. 21–3. *Ṣubḥ,* xiii, pp. 28–30. Ẓāhirī, p. 125, l. 7. *Taqwīm,* p. 245, l. 4.

[5] Cf. *Ṣubḥ,* xiv, p. 44, l. 9 ; p. 45, ll. 2–6 ; p. 46, ll. 2–4; and iv, p. 216, l. 7 ; p. 233, l. 11.

F

of the sixteenth century, the rents became again variable according to provinces and districts, and after the annexation of the military fiefs to the crown domains a fixed tribute was imposed on every village.[1] In practice, however, the lords maintained the *muqāsama*, and at the end of the eighteenth century they used to levy one-half or two-thirds of the crops.[2]

In Egypt the tenants of perpetually irrigated lands paid under the Mamlūks fixed and unchangeable yearly rents in money (*al-kharāj al-rātib*), and · an additional tax on the plantations of sugar-cane. The rents of the arable lands were levied according to their extent and quality, in Upper Egypt mostly in kind (up to three *irdabbs* of grain per *faddān*), in Lower Egypt mostly in money. The economic crisis which took place from 1384 to 1408, owing to the diminution of silver reserves and to the ensuing devaluation of the dirhem, resulted in a great increase of the cash rents.[3] The bad condition of peasantry was the cause of perpetual agrarian revolts [4] ; the Ottoman conquest made the things even worse,[5] and many peasants participated in 1523 in the revolt of Qānṣūh bey al-Muḥammadī, who tried to restore the Mamlūk state.[6] Between 1525–1535 the authorities gradually fixed the new nominal *kharāj* (*al-māl al-ḥurr*), a definite amount imposed on every *qīrāṭ* of a village and divided in a fixed manner into the *mīrī* and the legal *fā'iẓ*. Only this nominal sum was indicated in the charter (*taqsīṭ, sanad*) of a *multazim*, but the real *kharāj* was greater, and the additional

---

[1] Hammer, ii, p. 344 ; id., *Des Osm. Reichs Staatsverfassung und Staats-verwaltung*, i, pp. 180–327. Volney, ii, p. 373.

[2] Volney, ii, p. 374.

[3] Nuwayrī, viii, p. 249, ll. 3–11 ; p. 253, l. 10, to p. 255, l. 6 ; p. 261, l. 5. *Ṣubḥ*, iii, p. 453, l. 17, to p. 454, l. 13. *Nujūm*, vi, p. 69, l. 9. *Ḥawādith*, p. 655, ll. 1–8. *Ẓāhirī*, p. 97, l. 17 ; p. 108, l. 5.

[4] Poliak, *Les révoltes populaires en Égypte à l'époque des Mamelouks et leurs causes économiques* (*RÉI.*, 1934, pp. 251–273).

[5] A. de Kremer, *Notice sur Sha'rány* (*JA.*, 6ᵉ sér., xi, 1868), pp. 263–6. Ibn Iyās, v, p. 445, ll. 13–18 p. 452, ll. 12–14 ; p .466, ll. 16–18.

[6] Rustem, p. 68.

am●unt was denoted as *al-muḍāf wa-l-barrānī*.[1] The *kharāj*
and the *mīrī* were usually paid from the winter crops (except
in the rice plantations), and in Upper Egypt mostly in kind.[2]

The *kharāj* was not the only tax levied by the lords from
their serfs. Under the Mamlūks we find in Syria, Palestine
and the Lebanon' also (a) the tithe of the crops which remained
to the peasants after the *muqāsama* had been levied[3];
(b) gifts in kind at specified times of the year, *rasm al-a'yād
wa-l-khamīs*[4]; (c) the tax on the water-mills[5]; (d) various
local taxes.[6] In Egypt: (a) gifts in kind at specified times
of the year (*hadiyya, ḍiyāfa*), replaced in the domains of
al-khāṣṣ by a money tax[7]; (b) the tax for the annual
reparation of the local irrigating dams and canals[8]; (c) payments for pasture on uncultivated fields (a capitation
tax on the cattle, yearly rents or monthly payments)[9];

[1] Hammer, ii, pp. 40, 343. General Reynier, *De 'Élgypte après la bataille
d'Héliopolis* (quoted in *JA.*, 4ᵉ sér., i, 1843, pp. 165–8). Marcel, pp. 196–7,
206. Jabartī, iii, p. 251, l. 33; p. 267, ll. 16–17; iv, p. 74, l. 26; p. 101,
l. 13; p. 123, ll. 22–3; p. 142, l. 19; p. 209, l. 3; p. 221, l. 28.

[2] Lancret, *Mémoire sur le système d'imposition territoriale* (*Description
de l'Égypte, État Moderne*, i), pp. 246, 254. Jabartī, i, p. 318, ll. 24–8;
ii, p. 19, l. 12; p. 153, ll. 1, 2; p. 179, l. 19; p. 181, l. 30; p. 182, l. 2;
p. 193, l. 17. The expression " in money and in kind " is rendered by
Maqrīzī as *'ayn wa-ghalla* (*Khiṭaṭ*, i, p. 88, ll. 26, 32), by Jabartī as *al-māl
wa-l-ghilāl*, by Michael (p. 77, l. 3) as *ghirsh wa-dhakhā'ir* (in Egypt *dhakhīra*
= any payment, in grain or in money, sent from an estate to the lord:
Jabartī, i, p. 58, l. 3; p. 348, l. 21).

[3] Nuwayrī, viii, p. 259, ll. 7–14. Sometimes it was replaced by a fixed
tribute, and in the *waqf* lands and estates of pension it was not levied at all.

[4] Ibid., p. 245, l. 10, to p. 246, l. 1. In the domains of *al-khāṣṣ* it was
replaced by the duty of rendering hospitality to the rent-collectors during
three days (on the *qasm*, levy of *muqāsama*, cf. p. 258, ll. 10–11, and
Sakhāwī, viii, p. 106, l. 18).

[5] Nuwayrī, viii, p. 245, ll. 9–10.

[6] Ṣubḥ, xiii, p. 34, column 1, ll. 7–14; column 3, ll. 1–7, 14–19 (the
province of Tripoli).

[7] Nuwayrī, viii, p. 245, ll. 10–14. *Khiṭaṭ*, i, p. 88, ll. 28, 34; p. 90,
l. 16; p. 103, ll. 23–4. Ibn Iyās, iv, p. 207, ll. 3–5; v, p. 350, l. 11. *Nujūm*,
vi, p. 430, ll. 11–12.

[8] Ṣubḥ, iii, p. 449, ll. 4–19.
Nuwayrī, viii, p. 262, ll. 3–11.

(*d*) the tax on the fishes caught when water descends from the fields after the annual inundation of the Nile [1]; (*e*) a tenth of the produce of the date liquor (*'araq*) [2]; (*f*) *busuṭ*, probably a tax on the home-made carpets.[3] The following taxes were paid not only by the serf population but also by those inhabitants of the fief who did not derive their subsistence from agriculture and were not considered as the lord's serfs : (*a*) the taxes on commerce and industry, *mukūs* or *al-māl al-hilālī* [4]; (*b*) the capitation tax on the non-Moslems (*jawālī*), which prior to *al-rawk al-nāṣirī* was only occasionally conceded by the central government to the fief-holders, and afterwards always [5]; (*c*) sometimes specially favoured fief-holders were entitled to the heritages upon which there were no private legal claims.[6] In the Ottoman Syro-Palestinian military fiefs the additional taxes levied by the lords varied, as the *kharāj*, according to provinces and districts. In the crown domains the farmers were officially entitled to levy only those taxes which were enumerated in the charters delivered to them, e.g. the charters of the Syrian *muqāta'ajīs* mention the *mīrī*, the tax on the slaves (*'abūdiyya*), the house tax (*māl manzil*), the capitation tax on non-Moslems, light taxes on the *waqfs* and *tīmārs*, fines, and the extraordinary taxes imposed by the governor-general and levied through the medium of the *muqāta'ajīs*.[7]

That share of the produce which remained to the peasants was so small that they were always in debt. Under the Mamlūks they received every year from the lords loans of

---

[1] Nuwayrī, viii, p. 263, l. 3, to p. 264, l. 4.

[2] Ibid., p. 261, l. 6.

[3] Ibid.

[4] *Ṣubḥ*, iii, p. 471, ll. 4–9 (Egypt); xiii, p. 40, l. 11 (the province of Damascus). Ibn Duqmāq, v, p. 22, l. 2.

[5] *Sulūk*, II, i, p. 132. *Khiṭaṭ*, i, p. 88, l. 35 ; p. 90, ll. 8–11. *Ṣubḥ*, iii, p. 463, ll. 1–4. Nuwayrī, viii, p. 241, ll. 9–15.

[6] *Sulūk*, II, i, p. 132.

[7] Rustum, ii, pp. 24–6. The allegation of Volney (ii, p. 332), that the capitation tax was paid directly to the treasury and was not levied in the Lebanon is untrue (cf. Shidyāq, p. 110, l. 7 ; p. 112, l. 5).

grain (*al-taqāwī*), as seed and as food until the harvest.
The interest amounted to 10–11 per cent, though the lords
received for this purpose in their turn advances of grain
from the sultan.[1]   Under the Ottomans, in Egypt and
in the *pays abonnés* the peasants used to borrow working
cattle and grain from their lords, and in those parts of Syria
and Palestine where the annual *muqāṭaʻa* existed, from other
persons of wealth, in village and in town.[2] Towards the end
of the eighteenth century the Syrian peasants usually paid
12–30 per cent as interest, in about 1830 50 per cent for
fourteen months.[3]

Under the Mamlūks in Egypt only the perpetually irrigated
lands were held by the cultivators individually, and the
holders could convey them to their heirs and sell them.[4]
The arable lands were held in common, probably on the
same lines as in Syria and in Palestine until recent times :
each clan (*ḥamūla*) was entitled at the time of the annual
redivision of the common lands to a fixed share, and redivided
it among the clansmen according to the number of their
working cattle.[5]   The peasants without cattle automatically
became landless (*al-fallāḥūn al-baṭṭālūn*) ; in Lower Egypt
the sultans (till Barqūq) obliged such peasants to purchase
from the authorities the oxen which were previously employed
for the repairs of the irrigating dams.[6] It was the necessity
of ensuring a better supervision of small irrigating channels

---

[1] *Sulūk*, I, i, p. 141, n. 14.   *Khiṭaṭ*, i, p. 91, ll. 15–19.   Nuwayrī, viii,
p. 250, ll. 1–3 ;   p. 252, ll. 5–12 ;   p. 260, l. 1 ;   p. 278, ll. 7, 11.   Ibn ʻAbd
al-Ẓāhir, p. 55, l. 14.   *Ḥawādith*, p. 114, ll. 6–14 ;   p. 116, l. 18.

[2] *Recueil de Firmans*, p. 7, No. 22.   Roque, p. 79.   Volney, ii, pp. 167, 232.

[3] Volney, ii, p. 377.   M. Sabry, *L'Empire Égyptien sous Mohamed-Ali*,
Paris, 1930, p. 351.

[4] Nuwayrī, viii, p. 255, l. 2.

[5] Cf. Bergheim in *PEFQS.*, 1894, pp. 191–6, and Poliak in *JRAS.*,
1937, p. 105.   On the Egyptian village community in the seventh century,
cf. Ibn ʻAbd al-Ḥakam, *Futūḥ Miṣr* (Yale Oriental Series, iii), p. 153,
ll. 7–10.

[6] *Manhal*, ii, f. 75a, ll. 17–18.   In *Nujūm*, v, p. 600,
i, p. 316, l. 17, the text is defective.

through the personal responsibility of each peasant for a
specified portion of them that accelerated the dissolution
of the Egyptian village community.   Already under the
Mamlūks the common land was often divided by the lord's
clerks into several divisions (*qabā'il*, sing. *qibāla*), irrigated
by particular channels, and the rents were levied on each
division separately.[1]   The decisive step was the distribution
of the common lands of every village into fixed plots (*qīrāṭs*),
which replaced the village community as fiscal units (1526).
Whereas under the Mamlūks the fief-holder was responsible
for the annual repairs of the local irrigating dams and
canals, under the Ottomans this responsibility was imposed
on the peasants themselves.[2]   Therefore, while in Syria and
in Palestine the village community remained intact till the
sixties of the nineteenth century (and in many villages it
still exists, though every peasant has now a fixed and
transferable share), in Egypt at the end of the eighteenth
century the private holdings of peasants were already separated
by fixed boundary marks, except in some regions of Upper
Egypt, where the annual redivisions still existed, but every
member of the community had already a fixed share.[3]   The
disappearance of the land community increased the economical
differences among the peasants : whereas the village *shaykhs*
were exempt from the *mīrī* and often farmed the neighbouring
al-rizaq al-aḥbāsiyya, and seized the unowned lands in their
vicinity, so that their actual holdings amounted to 1,000
faddāns and more,[4] many other peasants became landless
agricultural workers,[5] especially because the *multazim* could
deprive those tenants who did not punctually pay the rents
of their holdings.

---

[1] Nuwayrī, viii, pp. 249–252. *Ṣubḥ*, iii, p. 458, ll. 7–17. *CIA.*, i, p. 358,
n. 14.

[2] Ẓāhirī, p. 129. *Ṣubḥ*, iii, p. 449. *Khiṭaṭ*, i, p. 101. Jabartī, iv, p. 293, l. 6.

[3] Reynier, loc. cit.

[4] Jabartī, i, p. 180, l. 26 ;   iv, p. 61, ll. 13–15 ;   p. 123, l. 32 ;   p. 209,
l. 27, to p. 210, l. 23.

[5] Ibid., iv, p. 274, ll. 10–28 ;   p. 293, ll. 9–10. Ryme, p. 27.

The Mamlūk feudatories often visited their fiefs, though usually stayed there but a short time.[1] Sometimes an emir appointed one of his mamlūks the permanent manager (*mutaḥaddith*) of his fief [2] or of one village only,[3] more often only a temporary envoy (*qāṣid*) for the levying of *kharāj* or some other purpose.[4] In Syria, Palestine, and the Lebanon, owing to the principle of *muqāsama*, the lord (or his representative) supervised the agricultural works of his tenants from the beginning to the end [5]; in Egypt he supervised only the use of the green manure, *takhdīr al-bilād*,[6] because on the lands so manured a considerably greater *kharāj* was levied.[7] The official minimum of cultivated area was the extent cultivated during the previous years; the rents per *faddān* were assessed after the *takhdīr*; and only in order to increase the rents, if possible, the lord's officials examined the changes brought about in the size of cultivable lands by the annual inundation of the Nile and the extent of the actually cultivated lands.[8] The rents were paid by every peasant directly to the officials of his lord, and not through the medium of the village community.[9] The lords could legally exploit their fiefs as they liked,[10] but the temporary character of the feudal land tenure prevented them for the most part

[1] Ibn Iyās, i, p. 244, l. 6; ii, p. 288, l. 4; p. 289, l. 1; iv, p. 104, ll. 17–18; p. 125, ll. 6–8; p. 429, ll. 19–21. *Ḥawādith*, p. 105, ll. 3–10; p. 459, l. 12. *Manhal*, i, f. 165a; ii, ff. 106a, 114b, 175b; iii, f. 106a; iv, f. 87a. *Sulūk*, I, ii, p. 27; II, i, p. 151. Ibn 'Abd al-Ẓāhir, p. 29, l. 13. Sakhāwī, ii, p. 275, l. 10.

[2] *Manhal*, i, f. 205a, l. 12; iii, f. 170b, l. 6.

[3] Then he was denoted as *shādd*: Sakhāwī, v, p. 266, l. 10; Ibn Iyās, iv, p. 271, ll. 17–19; v, p. 378, ll. 8–10.

[4] *Nujūm*, vi, p. 652, l. 1; p. 830, l. 19. *Ḥawādith*, p. 355, l. 3; p. 654, l. 8. Ibn Iyās, v, p. 80, l. 5; p. 130, l. 20.

[5] Nuwayrī, viii, p. 257, ll. 4–5; p. 258, ll. 3–10.

[6] *Ṣubḥ*, vi, p. 288, ll. 15–16; vii, p. 158, ll. 8–10. Nuwayrī, viii, p. 248, ll. 11–12; p. 249, l. 11, to p. 250, l. 1; p. 250, l. 9. *Ḥawādith*, p. 135, l. 5. Jabartī, iv, p. 293, l. 8.

[7] Cf. on the *bāq* lands: *Ṣubḥ*, iii, pp. 450, 454; *Khiṭaṭ*, i, p. 100, l. 28.

[8] Nuwayrī, viii, p. 249, l. 12, to p. 252, l. 3. *Ṣubḥ*, iii, p. 458, ll. 7–17.

[9] *Ḥawādith*, p. 654, ll. 4–22. *Nujūm*, vi, p. 399, l. 14–20.

[10] *Khiṭaṭ*, ii, p. 217, l. 31. *Ṣubḥ*, iv, p. 50, l. 8. *Daw' al-Ṣubḥ*, i, p. 258, l. 7.

from establishing demesne farms. The most frequent exceptions to this rule were the plantations of sugar-cane (owing to its rapid growth) and cattle breeding (the food of the mamlūks consisted mainly of meat and dairy produce). In the first case, at least, the forced labour of the serfs was employed.[1]

Under the *iltizām* system a portion of the estate was set apart for the demesne farm, and denoted as *ūsya* (in Arabized form *wasiya*), in the plural *awsiya* or *wasāyā*.[2] The demesne farm[3] was worked by servile labour.[4] The lands held by tenants were denoted as *ṭīn al-falāḥa*.[5] In addition to the permanent tenants, *muzāri'ūn*,[6] there were in Egypt also *shurakā'*, workers who cultivated the lord's land in return for a share of the produce, and who were liable to be deprived of their holdings whenever he wished.[7] In Syria and in Palestine only those farmers who were tribal chieftains had demesne farms. In the Lebanon all the farmers had them,[8] and the usual status of tenants there was that of the *shurakā'*.

The Mamlūk fief-holder was responsible to the sultan that the cultivated area would not be smaller at the end of his rule than at its beginning, and the sultan could give him concrete directions to this effect.[9] As in European

---

[1] *Ṣubḥ*, xiii, p. 34, col. 1, ll. 7–14. Ibn Iyās, i, p. 156, l. 20 ; p. 198, l. 11. *Manhal*, ii, f. 25a ; iii, f. 36a. Al-'Abbāsī, *Āthār al-Uwal*, p. 140.

[2] Jabartī, i, p. 51, l. 28 ; p. 184, ll. 9, 13 ; iv, p. 93, ll. 19, 30 ; p. 95, l. 22 ; p. 96, l. 5 ; p. 97, ll. 3, 4, 17, 23–7 ; p. 207, l. 10 ; p. 228, l. 25.

[3] Ibid., i, p. 343, ll. 27–8 ; p. 347, ll. 20–2 ; ii, p. 151, ll. 3–5 ; iii, p. 173, ll. 15–19 ; p. 175, ll. 20–7 ; p. 176, l. 4.

[4] Ibid., iii, p. 173, ll. 7–8 ; iv, p. 207, ll. 17–20.

[5] Ibid., iv, p. 81, l. 27 ; p. 209, ll. 3–4. *JA.*, 6e sér., xi, 1868, p. 265.

[6] Ibid., i, p. 345, ll. 2–3 ; iv, p. 60, l. 15 ; p. 154, ll. 2, 18, 22 ; p. 208, l. 25.

[7] Ibid., p. 344, l. 29 ; p. 349, l. 13 (cf. on Syria : *PEFQS.*, 1891, p. 105). In iv, p. 112, l. 2, and p. 191, l. 29, this term has the same meaning as in the Mamlūk sources : " the lords who possess portions of the same village."

[8] The al-Khāzins and Arslāns were denoted as " olive princes " (Mariti, p. 15 ; Michael, p. 109, l. 13).

[9] Ibn Iyās, iv, p. 104, ll. 17–18.

feudalism,[1] the central government was entitled to impose taxes (usually extraordinary) on the serfs of its vassals; these taxes always, directly or indirectly, diminished the revenues of the lords, and were therefore bitterly resented by them.[2] The same state of things existed under the Ottomans.

Among the *multazim's* officials we must mention his representative (*qā'imaqām*), who, in the village held by a single lord, was called *kāshif al-nāḥiya*; the Copt who supervised the collection of *kharāj* (*ṣarrāf*, *ṣayrafī*); the lord's special envoys (*mu'ayyanūn*); the guardian (*ghafīr*) of the demesne farm, and the *mushidd*, who probably supervised the servile labour.[3]

---

[1] Sir Paul Vinogradoff, *Feudalism* (*The Cambridge Medieval History*, iii), p. 479.

[2] Ibn Iyās, ii, pp. 252, 262, 302; iv, pp. 49, 153, 228, 291, 329, 333. *Qulūm al-kushshāf* (iv, p. 262, l. 11) = a tax for the district governors; *shiyākha* (iv, p. 262, 263, 390) = a tax levied by the authorities for the neighbour bedouin chieftains (cf. pp. 319, 354, 428).

[3] Jabartī, i, pp. 180–1, 305; iv, pp. 109, 207–8, 293.

VI. The End of Feudalism

With the invasion of Egypt by the French troops (1798),
the mamlūk rule in Lower Egypt came to an end. After the
return of the Ottomans (1801) Lower Egypt was occupied
by their Albanian mercenaries, whose commander,
Muḥammad 'Alī, became in 1805 the governor-general of
Egypt, and after 1813 [1] gradually created a new regular
army (*al-niẓām al-jadīd*), which was later recruited from
conscripts. The seven old regiments continued to receive
their allowances,[2] and their representatives in the *dīwān*
participated (together with the spiritual *shaykhs*) in the election
of Muḥammad 'Alī to the governor-generalship [3]; but in
1814 their privileges ceased to be hereditary, so that they
gradually vanished owing to the death of their members.[4]
At first the mamlūks remained lords of Upper Egypt (in
1803 some of their emirs even came into power in Cairo
for several months, but depended there on the Albanian
troops). In 1807 one of their commanders, Shāhīn bey al-Alfī,
seceded from them and was rewarded by Md. 'Alī with an
enormous *iltizām*, which contained the district of al-Fayyūm,
thirty villages in the district of al-Bahnasā, and ten in the
Giza district.[5] In 1811 Md. 'Alī destroyed the mamlūk corps :
Shāhīn bey and his troopers were executed, " the Southern
Emirs " and their mamlūks retreated to the Sudan, and
became owners of millet plantations there.[6] In 1816 they
were pardoned and gradually returned in small groups to
Egypt, where they received offices and pensions but not

---

[1] The first orders were issued on the 25th Sha'bān, A.H. 1230 (Jabartī, iv,
pp. 222 ff.). Two years later more vigorous steps were made.

[2] In 1801 the *jāmakiyya* was diminished by a third, and the *ghilāl al-
anbār* replaced by a money allowance (ibid., iii, p. 213, ll. 3–13).

[3] Ibid., iii, pp. 329–330.

[4] Ibid., iv, p. 256, ll. 27–8.

[5] Ibid., p. 73, ll. 7–11 ; p. 113, ll. 7–8 ; p. 116, ll. 26–9.

[6] Ibid., p. 264, l. 5.

lands.[1] In 1833–5 Md. 'Ali abolished the feudal military troops in Syria, Palestine, and the Lebanon : a forced disarmament of the population was carried out, no exception being made for the nobility, and conscription was introduced.[2] For several decades the farmers continued to employ mercenaries for the levying of taxes, but the regular troops were more numerous and better armed ; moreover, the mercenaries were now officially a part of the government forces, and were only temporarily lent to the farmers.[3]

The abolition of the feudal military forces was only a prelude to the abolition of the feudal land tenure. There were differences of opinion among the French authorities in Egypt whether the *iltizāms* should be reckoned feudal estates, like those abolished in France by the Revolution (this view was later enunciated by the General Reynier in his book, *De l'Égypte après la bataille d'Héliopolis*), or as allodial estates of their holders, whose right of property was afterwards limited by the Ottoman despotism.[4] The second opinion prevailed at first, because it seemed more likely to ensure the internal peace in the country and the support of the new regime by the spiritual *shaykhs*, and because too

---

[1] Ibid., pp. 246–7, 310, 317–18.

[2] Shidyāq, pp. 582–4. Michael, p. 55, l. 18. In the Lebanon a Christian militia was formed in 1835, and it soon became a more important political force than the disarmed nobility (Shidyāq, p. 585) : in 1840 it revolted against the emir (p. 589, ll. 6 ff.), and proclaimed a democratic political programme (p. 591, ll. 18–21), and after 1842 it delegated, in every village, the direction of guerrilla warfare against the Druses, to an elected chief (*shaykh al-shabāb*), not to a hereditary chieftain (p. 701, ll. 8–9).

[3] After 1778 the Syro-Palestinian mercenaries were known as " Hawwāra ", after the Egyptian bedouin tribe, though they were not necessarily Egyptians (*PEFQS.*, 1906, pp. 222–3, 288 ; Finn, i, pp. 166–171 ; Michael, pp. 46, 78 ; Shidyāq, p. 588). *Dulāt* (sing. *dālī[bāsh]*) and *lāwand* are older appellations (cf. Volney, ii, pp. 132–3). In the sixteenth and seventeenth centuries the usual term was *sagbān* or *sagmān*, " huntsmen " (Hammer, ii, p. 706 ; Shidyāq, pp. 131–3, 256 ff.).

[4] This view was afterwards accepted by de Sacy, *Sur la nature et sur les révolutions du droit de la propriété territoriale en Égypte* (*Mémoires de l'Institut de France*, 1818–1823), and contested by Worms in *JA.*, 1842–4. Napoleon could find it in Volney (i, p. 172), utilized by him as his manual.

radical reforms were liable to endanger the exportation of grain to France and the development of plantations of tropical plants.[1]   The *multazims* were made equal to the owners of allodial estates, and each of them received, after the scrutiny of his legal rights, a certificate (*garantie de propriété*) testifying that he is " the legitimate proprietor of his domain ".[2]   The mamlūk possessions in Lower Egypt and those estates the holders of which had not satisfactory title-deeds became national domains.[3]   The hopes connected with this agrarian policy were soon frustrated :   the sea blockade prevented any trade with France, and the peasant revolts compelled the French authorities to defend the *iltizām* system by military means.[4]   The last commander-in-chief, Menou (1800–1), showed himself therefore an adherent of the opposite policy, to enlarge the extent of the national domains through the gradual annexation of *iltizāms*.[5]

The Ottomans, after some hesitation,[6] restored the traditional *iltizām* system and abolished the national domains but put an end to the particular status of the *khazīnat band* lands.[7]   The increasing direct taxation of the peasants by the authorities,[8] the collection of the *mīrī* a half to two years

---

[1] These plans were the principal economic reasons of the French expedition.   Cf. Jabartī, iii, p. 4, l. 26 ;   p. 169, ll. 21–5 ;   Marcel, pp. 249–250 ; Ryme, pp. 9, 10, 29, 33, 85–6.

[2] Cf. P. G. Elgood, *Bonaparte's Adventure in Egypt*, Oxford, 1931, plate xiii ;   Jabartī, iii, p. 16, ll. 19–21 ;   p. 20, ll. 2–12 ;   p. 23, ll. 30–3.

[3] *Histoire Scientifique et Militaire de l'Expédition Française en Égypte*, iv, p. 92.   Jabartī, iii, p. 5, ll. 22–4 ;   p. 20, ll. 7–9 ;   p. 140, l. 24 (*aŧyān al-jumhūr*) ;   p. 154, l. 13 (*amlāk al-jumhūr*).

[4] Jabartī, iii, p. 30, l. 23 ;   p. 31, ll. 29–30 ;   Ryme, p. 73.

[5] Jabartī, iii, p. 139, l. 30, to p. 141, l. 8 ;   p. 179, ll. 20–2.   The income of the national domains was in 1800 thrice as great as in 1799, whereas the total state revenue sunk by more than a third (cf. Omar Toussoun, pp. 36–7).

[6] Jabartī, iii, p. 190, ll. 17–18 ;   p. 193, ll. 25–6 ;   p. 194, ll. 4–7 ;   p. 195, ll. 2–4 ;   p. 196, ll. 27–32 ;   p. 198, l. 6 ;   p. 202, l. 29.

[7] Ibid., iv, p. 94, ll. 9–20.

[8] Ibid., iii, pp. 234, 263, 269, 308–9, 313, 317, 319, 329, 338, 343–4 ; iv, pp. 7, 8, 14, 18, 69, 88–9, etc.

before the nominal time,[1] and the annual confiscations of a part of the *fā'iz* (since 1805) to meet the cost of the state troops and administration,[2] made, however, the traditional system more and more impracticable. In 1811 all the mamlūk *iltizāms* and most of other *iltizāms* in Upper Egypt (previously occupied by " the Southern Emirs ") were confiscated as spoil of war, *al-maḍbūṭ*.[3] In 1813, when the mercenary troops[4] fought in Arabia against the Wahhābīs, a decree was published confiscating all the *iltizāms* and compensating their holders by lifelong pensions equal to their former *fā'iz*.[5] After the return of the mercenaries this decree was amended : the *multazims* were given the right to receive, instead of pensions, their former *iltizāms* until their death, if they wished, but the extent of these *iltizāms* was diminished (owing to the diminution of the official *faddān* in the same year), the *mīrī* remained the same, and the *multazim* was entitled to levy *al-māl al-ḥurr* only.[6]

At the same time Muḥammad 'Alī abolished *al-rizaq al-aḥbāsiyya*,[7] so that Egypt became a single enormous *iltizām*,

[1] Ibid., ii, p. 179, l. 4 ; iii, p. 194, ll. 8–11 ; pp. 234, 288, 296, 326, 329, 347 ; iv, pp. 20, 69.

[2] Ibid., iii, p. 345, ll. 24–7 ; iv, pp. 10, 14, 60, 93, 95, 96, 97.

[3] Ibid., iv, p. 153, l. 27, to p. 154, l. 14 ; p. 183, ll. 27–9.

[4] Many Albanian mercenaries were then *multazims*, ibid., iii, p. 347, ll. 3–7 ; iv, p. 11, l. 17 ; p. 229, ll. 4–5.

[5] Ibid., iv, p. 203, l. 30, to p. 204, l. 18 ; p. 207, ll. 8–13 ; p. 222, ll. 6–8. Those *multazims* of Upper Egypt who were not implicated in the revolts of " the Southern Emirs " obtained a similar compensation in 1811, p. 154, l. 11. Prior to it Md. 'Alī sometimes settled in the same manner the cases of insolvent *multazims*, p. 109, ll. 30–1.

[6] Ibid., iv, p. 228, l. 4, to p. 229, l. 8 ; p. 256, ll. 27–8.

[7] In 1801 a small regular tax (*māl ḥimāya*) was imposed on them for the first time (Jabartī, iv, p. 94, ll. 30–3). In 1809 Md. 'Alī tried to impose the *mīrī* on these lands in al-Buḥayra (p. 93, ll. 17–26 ; p. 95, ll. 6, 22 ; p. 96, l. 5 ; p. 97, ll. 3–4, 17). In 1811 he became their exclusive farmer in Upper Egypt, imposed there on them a light *mīrī*, and somewhat diminished their extent (p. 141, l. 31, to p. 142, l. 4 ; p. 153, l. 29, to p. 154, l. 2 ; p. 183, to p. 184, l. 25). An additional diminution took place in all Egypt (p. 208, ll. 23–5 ; p. 209, ll. 4 ff.), and afterwards Md. 'Alī the remainder on the death of their beneficiaries (p. 256, ll. 25– and in Palestine they ceased to exist as a particular class of

farmed by its governor-general.[1] Only the allodial estates, *waqfs* (managed henceforth by him) and *ūsyas* (retained by the former *multazims*)[2] had a particular status. The holders of other lands were in the same position as the holders of *ṭīn al-falāḥa* under the *iltizām* system : they could alienate and purchase lands, but the lord was entitled to order what crops they had to cultivate, to purchase all their produce and to deprive the dilatory *kharāj*-payers of their holdings. As, however, the successors of Md. 'Alī gave up his policy of severe control and monopolies, many lands were acquired by non-cultivators (who did not necessarily belong to the old feudal class), and the taxation of the kharājī lands gradually became similar to that of the allodial,[3] the Khedive's tenants[4] gradually became landed proprietors. The separation of the Khedive's private budget from the state budget in 1879, owing to the establishment of the civil list, and the cessation of the tribute to the Ottoman Empire in 1914 put an end to the last lawful vestiges of the feudal system in Egypt.

In Syria and in Palestine the abolition of the farming of the crown domains was inaugurated by Md. 'Alī in 1838,[5] and

---

lands after the Ottoman conquest, and became the nucleus of the local *waqf ghayr ṣaḥīḥ*, viz. these " tribute-paying " lands the revenues of which are set apart by the state for some pious purpose (to-day they form the bulk of the local *waqfs*). The necessity of meeting the cost of the army, which was the official reason for the abolition of *al-rizaq al-aḥbāsiyya* in Egypt (ibid., p. 184, ll. 11–12), recalls the frequent attempts of the Mamlūk sultans to abolish the *waqfs* and to divide them into military fiefs ; under the pressure of the religious administration they contented themselves with temporary confiscation of the *waqfs'* revenues (Ibn Iyās, i, pp. 267, 330 ; ii, pp. 97, 257, 268–9 ; iv, pp. 14–15, 18 ; v, pp. 124, 173 ; *Nujūm*, vi, pp. 47, 69 ; *Ḥawādith*, p. 636).

Jabartī (iv, p. 242, l. 1), calls him *ḥākim Miṣr wa-ṣāḥibuhā wa-iqṭā'ihā* [*sic*].

[2] Ibid., p. 207, ll. 10–11 ; p. 228, ll. 24–8.

[3] Cf. Cromer, pp. 23, 89, 90, 94, 132.

[4] Cf. Jabartī, iv, p. 207, l. 13: *fallāḥīn al-bāshā* (colloq.) = the pasha's serfs.

[5] Cf. Rustum, iii–iv, pp. 76–9 (particularly

in the following year it was proclaimed by the sultan throughout the Empire.   The old lords retained the lands cultivated by their workers and *shurakā'* ;   the lands cultivated by permanent settlers were now held by the village communities directly from the crown. The levying of the *mīrī*, gradually replaced by the tithe,[1] was annually farmed, and the farmer of a village (or a group of villages) was not infrequently the former lord ; however, he had legal authority over the village only during the tax collection, though in practice (especially in the case of a tribal chieftain) his position was often the same as before.[2] In Jabal al-Durūz the family of al-Aṭrash remained lords of all the lands ·till the agrarian revolution of 1886–7, when in every village one-quarter to one-eighth of lands were allotted to the local chieftains and the remainder to the common peasants.[3] At the time of the compulsory registration of lands (*taṭwīb*), which began in 1860 and continued until the commencement of the twentieth century, the common lands were divided into private holdings, and their holders received the right to alienate them to townsmen and residents of other villages ; in many villages, however, the communal tenure remained, and the lands were fictitiously registered in the name of four or five notables.[4] The uncultivated lands were purchased

---

[1] During the period of transition the peasants had to pay both taxes. In 1894 the *mīrī* (then a pecuniary tax, 3–5 per cent on the valuation of lands), was paid by the village community directly to the treasury, and the tithe (levied then in kind) was farmed, the tax-farmer collecting in practice 33 per cent of the crops instead of 10 per cent, Bergheim in *PEFQS.*, 1894, pp. 197–8.

[2] Cf. Finn, i, pp. 228–235, 305–7, 316.

[3] Bouron, pp. 214–15, 333–4. Cf. A. J. Toynbee, *The Islamic World since the Peace Settlement*, Oxford, 1927, p. 408.

[4] *PEFQS.*, 1891, p. 105 ; 1894, p. 195. L. Oliphant, *The Land of Gilead*, N.Y., 1881, pp. 86, 184, 248. H. C. Luke and E. Keith-Roach, *The Handbook of Palestine*, 3rd ed., pp. 261–2. According to G. Dalman, *Arbeit und Sitte in Palästina*, ii, 1932, p. 36, the *taṭwīb* began in 1863. Since then the title-deed of a landholder has been known as *qūshān*. The former *muqāṭa'ajīs* received two charters : *sharṭ-nāma* from the superior (Rustum, ii, p. 25, l. 11 ; p. 53, l. 9), and *ḥujja* from the *qāḍī* (cf. the examples, ibid., i, pp. 121–3 ; ii, pp. 24–6, 69–70).

from the treasury by persons of wealth and influence, many of whom were state officials (hence the term " effendi " became in the colloquial language a synonym of " estate-owner "). This fate was shared by the villages which were founded subsequent to the domination of Md. 'Alī. (1831–1841) and were not registered by the Turkish authorities.[1] As the old villages were concentrated for the most part in the hill districts,[2] it was the plains and the regions on the confines of the desert (as the Hauran and the Negeb) which became the principal zones of great estates.[3]

In the Lebanon the most important dates in the fight against feudalism were : the abolition of the inequality of the *mīrī* payments in 1844–8 [4] ; the limitation of the power of the *muqāṭa'ajīs* in 1845, when in the mixed Druso-Christian districts every *muqāṭa'ajī* was compelled to share his authority with an " agent " belonging to the other community ; the peasant revolt of 1854, which put an end to the prerogatives of the nobility in the North Lebanon,[5] and the Lebanese constitution (*Réglement organique*) of 1861–4, which proclaimed in its 6th art. the " equality of all before the law, abolition of all feudal privileges, and notably of those of the *muqāṭa'ajīs* ". The Lebanon remained an autonomous tributary state within the Ottoman Empire, but its governor (a non-Lebanese Ottoman Christian) and his district agents were no longer farmers of the tribute but salaried officials. This constitution (which remained in force

---

[1] The registers of *mīrī*-paying villages, arranged under Md. 'Alī, were not revised till the *taṭwīb*, Finn, i, p. 172. Cf. on the plain of Esdraelon, Oliphant, pp. 277–8.

[2] Because of greater security from nomads and mercenary troops, Mariti, p. 164 ; Volney, ii, pp. 68, 336–7. The sea-coast was depopulated by the Mamlūks in 1291, in order to prevent the future Crusaders from using it as military base, A. F., iv, p. 26, l. 31 ; Anonym, p. 23, l. 12.

[3] *PEFQS.*, 1891, pp. 104–5. Auhagen, *Beiträge zur Kenntnis der Landes-natur und der Landwirtschaft Syriens*, Berlin, 1907, p. 52.

[4] Shidyāq, p. 701, ll. 13 ff. ; p. 718, ll. 4–7, 18 ff.

[5] Cf. H. Lammens, *La Syrie*, Beirut, 1921, ii, p. 177.

until the World War) still made considerable concessions to the old feudal families : the governor, when appointing a district agent, had to take in account " the importance of his property " (art. 3), and the district administrative councils represented " the various elements of the population and the interests of the landowners " (art. 4).

The abolition of serfdom was also a gradual process. Already in 1811 Muḥammad 'Alī gave to the serfs of the *multazims* the right to lay plaints against their lords before the office established especially for this purpose.[1] The interdiction to leave the village without the lord's permission remained,[2] and was even among the causes of the Egypto-Ottoman war of 1831–3.[3] It was, however, denounced then by the sultan as illegal,[4] discontinued in Syria and in Palestine after their reconquest by the Ottomans (considerably assisted by the peasant rebels), and came to an end in Egypt when the successors of Muḥammad 'Alī gave up his policy of severe control of the economic activities of the peasants. In the Lebanon serfdom was usually milder than in the neighbouring countries, owing to the tribal connection between the lord and the serf ; in the North it was abolished by the revolt of 1854, in the South by the constitution of 1861–4.

---

[1] Jabartī, iv, p. 138, ll. 15–32.

[2] Ibid., p. 81, l. 22 ; p. 207, l. 16. Rustum (*advance notice*, 1928), p. 12.

[3] It is not clear whether the final motive was (as Olberg, pp. 56–7, and other contemporary writers say), the refusal of the governor-general of Acre to deliver fugitive Egyptian peasants to their master, Md. 'Alī, or (as A. J. Rustum says in *The Royal Archives of Egypt and the Origins of the Egyptian Expedition to Syria*, Beirut, 1936, pp. 25–6), the refusal of their new lords (the village *shaykhs*) to permit those of them who wished to return to Egypt to do so.

[4] Olberg, p. 57.

INDEX OF FEUDAL FAMILIES

INDEX OF TECHNICAL TERMS

‘abīd, 2
‘abūdiyya, 68
aghā, pl. aghawāt, 3, 6, 54
afandī, 60 (cf. 80)
ahbās, 32–4
‘alāma, 30, 31
‘āmil, pl. ‘ummāl, 45, 47
amīr (akhūr kabīr), 3●, (al-khazna), 49, (al-malā’), 10, (al-Ṣa‘īd), 50
‘aqārāt, 58
aqāṭi‘ sulṭāniyya, 18, 46
aqcha, 42
‘araq, 68
arpaliq, 52
ashāb al-‘atāmina, 53
‘ashīr (‘ashā’ir), al-, 11, 12
atābak, 14, (al-‘asākir), 1
aṭyān al-jumhūr, 76
awlād al-nās, 10, 14, 29, 33, 38, 40, 54
a‘yān, 58
‘azab, 53
baḥriyya, al , 2
baklīk, pl. bakālīk, 58
balāṣiyya, 14
banū l-atrāk, 14
bāq, 71
bāsh, 2
baṭṭāl, 32
baylarbay, 55
bayt al-māl, 36
bilād al-sulṭāniyya, al-, 46
buluk, 53
būq wa-l-‘alam, al-, 31, 54
busuṭ, 68
ḍaḥāyā, 4
dālī [bāsh], pl. dulāt, 75
dallāl al-iqṭā‘āt, 29
ḍamān, 45
darak, 9, (ṣāḥib al-), 60
dār al-ḥarb, 44
dār al-sa‘āda, 46
dawra, 63
dhakhīra, 67
dhimma, 48
dihqān, 58
dimūz, 47
dīnār jayshī, 8, 21
dīwān, 49, 50, 53, 61, 62, 74, (al-aḥbās), 34, (al-badal, al-badhl), 29, (al-dawla), 4, 18, 25, 45, (al-dhakhīra), 22, 25, 45, (al-inshā’), 30, 31, (al-iqṭā‘, al-jaysh),

20–3, 30–3, 40, (al-khāṣṣ), 5, 24, 25, 45, (al-mufrad), 4, 6, 8, 18, 25, 45, 47, (al-murtaja‘), 22, (al-musta’jarāt wa-l-ḥimāyāt), 25, (al-sulṭān), 22, (al-ustādāriyya), 4, (al-wizāra), 4, 7
ḍiyāfa, 67
faddān, 5, 33, 34, 61, 66, 70, 71, 77
fā’iẓ (fāīẓ), al-, 49, 66, 77
falāḥa, 64
fallāḥ qarārī (qarrār), 64
fallāḥīn al-bāshā, 78
fallāḥūn al-baṭṭālūn, al-, 69
faṣl, 45, 48
fawāris, 3
fay’, 23
fighār, 61
furad (furaḍ), 50
furūsiyya (anwā’, funūn, ‘ilm al-), 15
futuwwa, al-, 15
gamulyān, 40, 53
ghafīr, 73
ghāya, 51
ghilāl al-anbār (al-shuwan), 53, 74
ghilmān, 2, (sulṭāniyya), 14
ghuzāt, 14
ghuzz, al-, 54
gönüllü, 53
hadiyya, 67
ḥājib, pl. ḥujjāb, 14, 15, 65
ḥalqa, ajnād al-, 2, 3, 5–10, 13, 16, 19, 21, 24, 27–9, 31, 33, 40
ḥamūla, 69
ḥāṣil, 42, 43
ḥimāya, 25
ḥiṣṣa, pl. ḥiṣaṣ, 50
ḥujja, 79
ḥulwān, 62
‘ibra, 21, 23–5, 27
iijār, 61
ikhtiyāriyya, 53
iltizām, 48, 50, 54, 55, 61, 62, 72, 74–8
‘imāma, 15
inkishāriyya, 53
iqṭā‘, pl. iqṭā‘āt, aqāṭi‘, 18, 35, 41, 48, 50, (al-khilāfa), 35
irdabb, 46, 66
iṣbāhiyya, iṣbahāniyya, 53
ishhād, 30, 31
iṭlāq-āt, 5
jabalū, 42
jāmakiyya, 4, 53, 74

NOTE.—Arabic sources of the period treated in this survey substitute one of the letters *th-t-ṭ* and *dh-d* by another, e.g. *aṭābak* (Ibn Taghrī Birdī), *dakhīra* (Ibn Iyās). Arabic characters in Turkish words were pronounced by the Arabs as in Arabic.

www.ingramcontent.com/pod-product-compliance
Lightning Source LLC
Chambersburg PA
CBHW061701130726
47996CB00006B/2115